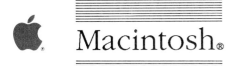

Macintosh® Designing Cards and Drivers for Macintosh II and Macintosh SE

Addison-Wesley Publishing Company, Inc.
Reading, Massachusetts   Menlo Park, California   New York
Don Mills, Ontario Wokingham, England Amsterdam   Bonn
Sydney Singapore Tokyo Madrid San Juan

Simultaneously published in the United States and Canada.

ISBN 0-201-19256-X
BCDEFGHIJ-DO-898
Second Printing, March 1988

Contents

Part II The Macintosh SE Interface II-1

Figures and tables

Preface

About This Book

This book is really two books in one. Part I applies to the Apple® Macintosh® II computer with its NuBus interface between the MC68020 processor and the expansion cards inserted in NuBus slots. Part II is devoted to the Apple Macintosh SE computer with its SE-Bus interface between the MC68000 processor and an expansion card inserted into the expansion connector. Each part provides information that you will need to develop expansion cards and device drivers for these computers.

Design philosophy

In keeping with the Macintosh design philosophy, it is incumbent upon you, the card designer and driver writer, to make the installation of the card and its use by applications as transparent as possible. To the greatest extent possible, an application should rely on only a few high-level calls (if any) and not have to use low-level calls. To do otherwise jeopardizes the broadest potential use of your product.

Notation conventions

Throughout Part I, on the Macintosh II, a NuBus word means a 32-bit word and a NuBus halfword is 16 bits wide. In Part II, on the Macintosh SE, a word is 16 bits wide and a longword contains 32 bits. This usage is consistent with the Texas Instruments specification of the NuBus and the Motorola documentation of the MC68000 microprocessor.

Address ranges are given as "*lower address* through *higher address*" or "*lower address–upper address*"; in either form the range is inclusive of the given endpoints. For example, an access range in memory is given in text as "$00 0000 through $3F FFFF," and in a table as "$00 0000–$3F FFFF."

A preceding slash is used to designate an active-low signal, for example, /ACK. A range of signals is designated like this, with the highest numbered signal first: /AD31–/AD0. If there is more than one subrange in a set, the subranges are enclosed in angle brackets like this: </AD31–/AD29, /AD7–/AD0>.

Macintosh resource types are designated by enclosing them in single straight quotation marks, for example, 'INIT'.

The term *processor* is often used instead of microprocessor or CPU. The processor usually refers to the microprocessor on the main logic board and *coprocessor* refers to another processor on an expansion card.

The following abbreviations are used:

kilobyte   K
kilobit   Kbit
megabyte   MB
megabit   Mbit
gigabyte   GB

The distinction between boards and cards is as follows: boards are a permanent part of the computer (for example, the main logic board), whereas cards are insertable and capable of being added or exchanged to accomplish functional expansion or reconfiguration of the system.

Aids to understanding

The first time a specialized term appears in this manual it is printed in **boldface.** All such terms are defined in the glossary at the back of the book.

❖ *Note:* A note like this usually contains information that is interesting but not essential for an understanding of the main text.

Warning
Warnings like this indicate potential problems.

Mechanical drawings and design guides

Mechanical drawings of cards and connectors are provided in Chapters 7, 14, and 15. These drawings are design guides used within Apple Computer and were correct at the time of publication. Future updates to this manual and to the drawings may be made available through APDA™, the Apple Programmer's and Developer's Association.

APDA is an excellent source of technical information for anyone interested in developing Apple-compatible products. Membership in the association allows you to purchase Apple technical documentation, programming tools, and utilities. For information on membership fees, available products, and prices, please contact

APDA
290 SW 43rd Street
Renton, WA 98055
(206) 251-6548
AppleLink: APDA
MCI: 312-7449
CompuServe #73527,27

About the Macintosh technical documentation

Apple Computer has produced several books that explain the hardware and software of the Macintosh family of computers. There are *Inside Macintosh*, Volumes I through V, books about single aspects of the Macintosh, introductory books, and Macintosh-related books.

The original Macintosh documentation consisted solely of the noble tome *Inside Macintosh*, a three-volume compendium covering the whole of the Macintosh Toolbox and Operating System for the original 64K Macintosh ROM, together with user interface guidelines and hardware information. With the introduction of the Macintosh Plus (128K ROM), Volume IV of *Inside Macintosh* was released. A fifth volume has now been added, covering the Macintosh SE and Macintosh II computers (both containing 256K of ROM). Volumes IV and V are delta guides; that is, they explain only what is different about the new machines. Taken all together, the five volumes of *Inside Macintosh* provide a comprehensive reference for the Macintosh family of computers.

With the growth of the Macintosh family, some of the material in *Inside Macintosh* is starting to appear in single-subject books. Each of those books provides complete information about its subject, including information that may appear in one or more volumes of *Inside Macintosh*.

For people who are new to the Macintosh world, Apple has created two introductory books: *Technical Introduction to the Macintosh Family* and *Programmer's Introduction to the Macintosh Family*. These books provide explanations and guidelines for using the features described in *Inside Macintosh*.

In addition to the books about the Macintosh itself, there are books on related subjects, including books about the user interface and Apple's floating-point numerics, and the reference books for the Macintosh Programmer's Workshop.

Table P-1 gives a brief description of each of the books in the Macintosh technical documentation. Figure P-1 is a roadmap to the Macintosh technical documentation. Starting with *Technical Introduction to the Macintosh Family,* the paths in the roadmap show the relationships among the books. For example, it's logical to read *Programmer's Introduction to the Macintosh Family* before *Inside Macintosh.*

Table P-1
Macintosh technical documentation

Original *Inside Macintosh*	
Inside Macintosh, Volumes I–III	Complete reference to the Macintosh Toolbox and Operating System for the original 64K ROM
Inside Macintosh, Volume IV	Delta guide to the Macintosh Plus (128K ROM)
Inside Macintosh, Volume V	Delta guide to the Macintosh SE and Macintosh II (256K ROM)
Introductory books	
Technical Introduction to the Macintosh Family	Introduction to the Macintosh software and hardware for all Macintosh computers: the original Macintosh, the Macintosh Plus, the Macintosh SE, and the Macintosh II
Programmer's Introduction to the Macintosh Family	Introduction to programming the Macintosh system for programmers who are new to it
Single-subject books	
Macintosh Family Hardware Reference	Reference to the Macintosh hardware for all Macintosh computers, excluding the Macintosh XL
Designing Cards and Drivers for Macintosh II and Macintosh SE	Hardware and device driver reference to the expansion capabilities of the Macintosh II and Macintosh SE
Related books	
Human Interface Guidelines: The Apple Desktop Interface	Detailed guidelines for developers implementing the Macintosh user interface
Apple Numerics Manual	Description of the Standard Apple Numerics Environment (SANE), an IEEE-standard floating-point environment supported by all Apple computers
Macintosh Programmer's Workshop 2.0 Reference	Description of the Macintosh Programmer's Workshop (MPW), Apple's software development environment for all Macintosh computers

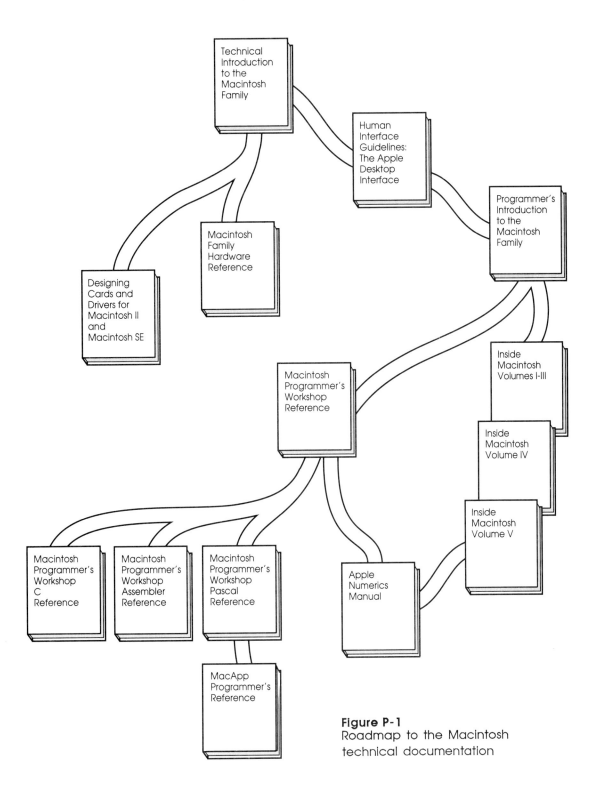

Figure P-1
Roadmap to the Macintosh
technical documentation

Part I

The Macintosh II Interface

Introduction

About Part I

The Apple implementation of NuBus is the subject of Part I of this book; that implementation is an extension of the Texas Instruments product documented in their NuBus Specification, document number TI-2242825-0001*A, copyright 1983. Some features of NuBus, most notably block data transfer and system parity valid, are documented for completeness even though not supported in the Macintosh II; these instances are clearly labeled.

Chapter 1 provides a block diagram of the complete Macintosh II main logic board and an overview of computer operation. The chapter then describes the NuBus interface architecture and the state machines used to implement it.

Chapter 2 describes NuBus features, provides a simplified diagram of the NuBus hardware, defines many NuBus terms, classifies the signals used to implement communication over the bus, and discusses the most basic timing and transaction cycle relationships.

Chapter 3 details each signal, its timing, and its line characteristics. The chapter defines various types of bus cycles, then describes the sequential combination of bus cycles to perform transactions.

Chapter 4 describes how cards inserted in NuBus slots can access memory in the Macintosh II.

Chapter 5 gives the rules for arbitration to resolve the contention between cards for bus mastership so that all cards have access to the bus data transfer capacity.

Chapter 6 provides an electrical design guide for NuBus expansion cards, focusing on the capabilities required of line drivers and receivers.

Chapter 7 provides a physical design guide for NuBus expansion cards. Guidelines for the mechanical and thermal design are followed by product safety recommendations.

Chapter 8 defines the firmware data structures typically stored on the card in ROM.

Chapter 9 describes several driver options, driver installation, and the video driver declaration ROM and routines. Pseudo code for an actual video card driver is provided.

Chapter 10 contains design examples, including schematics and PAL equations for two NuBus cards that have been built and tested.

Chapter 11 concludes Part I of the book with a description of the Macintosh II Video Card.

Appendix A, which follows Part II, contains the PAL listings for the NuBus Test Card described in Chapter 10.

Appendix B contains the PAL listings for the SCSI-NuBus Test Card described in Chapter 10.

Addressing design philosophy

Whenever possible, use 32-bit addressing conventions and methods. This is your best guarantee of future software compatibility.

Notation conventions

Throughout Part I a NuBus word means a 32-bit word and a NuBus halfword is 16 bits wide. This usage is consistent with the Texas Instruments specification of the NuBus.

A slash preceding the letters of a signal name indicates an active-low signal, for example, /START. Another commonly used designation for the same signal is START*.

Use of NuBus

NuBus is a trademark of Texas Instruments, Inc. Part I of this book describes the implementation of NuBus by Apple Computer in the Macintosh II. Certain features of the NuBus are not implemented in the Macintosh II but may be in future products; note is made of that fact where appropriate.

The Institute of Electrical and Electronics Engineers (IEEE) standard, *IEEE 1196, NuBus—A Simple 32-Bit Backplane Bus,* may be ordered from

Institute of Electrical and Electronics Engineers
345 East 47 Street
New York, NY 10017

NuBus licensing requirements

Texas Instruments owns patents on the NuBus. Those who wish to make devices that will interface with NuBus machines will need to obtain a license directly from Texas Instruments. For further details please send your request to

Texas Instruments, Inc.
12501 Research Boulevard
Austin, TX 78759
Attention: NuBus Licensing
M/S 2151

Chapter 1

The Macintosh II Architecture

This chapter provides a basic description of the structure and organization of the Macintosh II computer. The I/O bus used for expansion of the Macintosh II beyond the capabilities of the ports (connectors) on the back of the machine is based on the Texas Instruments NuBus. The chapter places the NuBus interface in context within the total computing machine. NuBus slots truly make the Macintosh II an open Macintosh and allow a wide variety of devices to be connected to the computer.

Overview of the hardware

Features of the Macintosh II are

□ 800K internal 3.5-inch floppy disk drive

□ optional internal 20, 40, or 80 MB, half-high 5.25-inch SCSI hard disk and an optional second 800K internal floppy disk drive (up to six external drives may be connected to the SCSI port at the back of the computer)

□ 16 MHz MC68020 processor, compatible with other Macintosh timing and software

□ 256K ROM

□ 1 MB RAM, expandable to 2 MB with 256 Kbit chips, or to 8 MB with 1M bit chips (over 2 GB available through NuBus slots)

□ six NuBus expansion slots supporting 32-bits of address and data

□ two mini-8 connectors that are for serial ports supporting RS-232 and AppleTalk®

□ optional MC68851 paged memory management unit (PMMU) allows true 32-bit address translation with hardware page replacement

□ standard MC68881 floating-point coprocessor allows high speed, high accuracy computation to IEEE standards

□ Apple Desktop Bus™ (ADB) supporting mouse and ADB keyboard with built-in cursor keys and numeric keypad; allows additional input devices (graphics tablet, for example)

□ keyboard power-on and software power-off help ensure data integrity on disk (power may be controlled from a NuBus card)

□ multiple display options available because video card is in NuBus slot (12-inch and 19-inch black-and-white, and 13-inch color monitors are available)

□ Apple Sound Chip provides four-voice synthesis in hardware, one channel through internal speaker, and stereo sound through jack at rear of cabinet

□ long-life lithium battery for clock and calendar

□ external connectors: two serial port connectors, two Apple Desktop Bus connectors, a SCSI connector, six NuBus slots (one connector for each card in a slot), and a stereo sound jack

Hardware architecture

The following discussion is brief and intended only to show the place of the NuBus in the computer architecture. For a complete description of hardware operation, see the *Macintosh Family Hardware Reference* manual. The *Technical Introduction to the Macintosh Family* contains a higher level overview.

A block diagram of the Macintosh II computer is shown in Figure 1-1. The Macintosh II contains a Motorola MC68020 microprocessor driven by a 15.6672 megahertz (MHz) clock. Memory consists of random access memory (RAM) and read-only memory (ROM).

Several chips enable the microprocessor to communicate with external devices. There are six I/O devices shown in the diagram:

☐ a 65C23 Versatile Interface Adapter (VIA1) for communicating with the ADB transceiver which, in turn, communicates with the mouse and keyboard (the VIA also communicates with the real time clock—RTC)

☐ another 65C23 Versatile Interface Adapter (VIA2) for handling interrupts from the NuBus slots

☐ an NCR 53C80 SCSI (Small Computer System Interface) for high-speed data transfer with the optional internal hard disk and any other SCSI device

☐ a Zilog Z8530 Serial Communications Controller (SCC) for serial communication

☐ an Apple custom chip, called the IWM (Integrated Woz Machine), for 3.5-inch floppy disk drive control

☐ the Apple Sound Chip (ASC) sound generator

The interface with the video display is through the NuBus to a video card in one of the slots.

The MC68881 floating-point numerics processor uses the coprocessor interface of the MC68020.

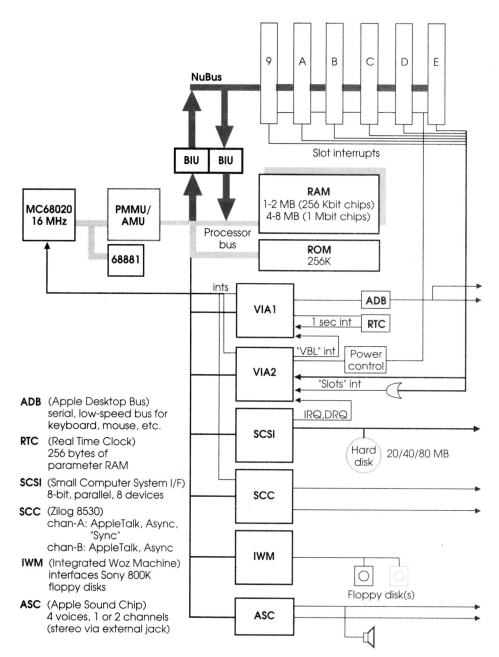

ADB (Apple Desktop Bus)
serial, low-speed bus for
keyboard, mouse, etc.

RTC (Real Time Clock)
256 bytes of
parameter RAM

SCSI (Small Computer System I/F)
8-bit, parallel, 8 devices

SCC (Zilog 8530)
chan-A: AppleTalk, Async,
"Sync"
chan-B: AppleTalk, Async

IWM (Integrated Woz Machine)
interfaces Sony 800K
floppy disks

ASC (Apple Sound Chip)
4 voices, 1 or 2 channels
(stereo via external jack)

Figure 1-1
Block diagram of the Macintosh II

RAM

RAM is the working memory of the system. Its base address is $00. The first 256 bytes of RAM (addresses $00 through $FF) are normally used by the MC68020 as exception vectors; these are the addresses of the routines that gain control whenever an exception such as an interrupt or a trap occurs. RAM also contains the system and application heaps, the stack, and other information used by applications.

The MC68020 accesses to Macintosh II RAM are *not* interleaved (alternated) with the video display's accesses during the active portion of a screen scan line; this is different from the Macintosh, Macintosh Plus, and Macintosh SE. Video RAM is located on the video card inserted in a NuBus slot. The MC68020 has uninterrupted access to RAM, making the average RAM 32-bit access rate equal to 3.13 MHz.

ROM

ROM is the system's permanent read-only memory. Its base address is available as the constant romStart and is also stored in the global variable ROMBase. ROM contains the routines for the Toolbox and Operating System, and the various system traps.

Device I/O

The Macintosh II uses memory-mapped I/O, which means that each device in the system (a peripheral to the processor) is accessed by reading or writing to specific locations in the address space of the computer. The address space reserved for device I/O contains blocks devoted to each of the devices within the computer. Each device contains logic that recognizes when it's being accessed, and the device responds in the appropriate manner.

For compatibility with MC68000-based Macintosh computers, the Macintosh Operating System operates by default in 24-bit mode. New applications running under the current Macintosh Operating System can take advantage of the full 32-bit mode for slot access as explained in Chapter 4.

Separate address spaces are reserved for accessing cards in NuBus slots. For a device in NuBus slot number s (where s is a constant in the range $9 through $E), the address space begins at address $Fs00 0000 and continues through the highest address, at $FsFF FFFF.

The MC68020 can directly access 2^{32} or 4 gigabytes of address space. In the Macintosh II, this is partially accessible with the Macintosh Operating System in 24-bit mode or totally accessible in 32-bit mode.

In general, ROM routines won't run in 32-bit mode under the current Macintosh Operating System. An application written to run in 32-bit mode must switch to 24-bit mode before calling any ROM routine and return to 32-bit mode thereafter.

If an application needs to access a NuBus card in 32-bit mode (because it needs to access more than 1MB of slot space, for example), you can use the system call SwapMMUMode to perform mode switching. This call is described in *Inside Macintosh,* Volume V, Chapter 33, "Operating System Utilities."

The A/UX® operating system runs entirely in 32-bit mode.

The standard memory management unit is the Address Mapping Unit (AMU); it accomplishes a 24 to 32-bit memory mapping translation. The mode change is controlled by a bit in VIA2. This method offers the direct use of all 32 bits in one mode and a mapped set of addresses in 24-bit mode. A more capable but more expensive option is the paged memory management unit (PMMU). The PMMU is also capable of ignoring the high eight bits of the address in order for the Macintosh Operating System to run in 24-bit mode.

Chapter 4, "Access to Address Space," shows in detail how the address space is allocated.

Address/data bus

Figure 1-2 displays the architecture of the address/data buses in the Macintosh II. Note that the address and data buses are separate on the MC68020 processor side of the NuBus interface (transceivers and control), and that the addresses and data are multiplexed on the NuBus side of the interface. Of primary interest in Figure 1-2 are

□ the address and data paths (shown grayed) to and from the NuBus transceivers

□ the paths from NuBus control, carrying the utility, control, arbitration, and slot ID signals (these signals are listed in Table 2-2)

The 32-bit wide multiplexed address or data bus connects to the six slot connectors as shown. See the section "Address/Data Signals" in Chapter 3 for a description of the address/data bus.

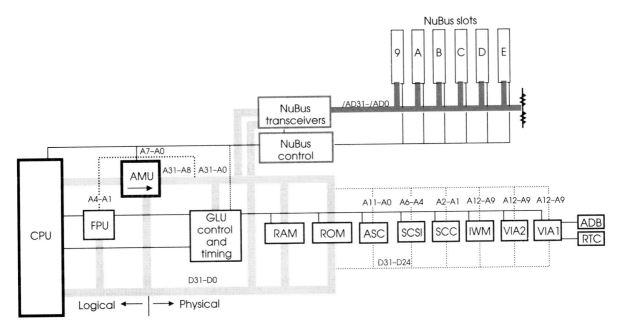

Figure 1-2
Address/data bus architecture

NuBus interface architecture

The NuBus interface at the top of Figure 1-1 shows bidirectional bus interface unit (BIU) blocks between the MC68020 bus and the NuBus. Figure 1-3 shows a further breakdown of the functional elements inside the BIU.

The BIU is implemented as four state machines, three of which are shown in Figure 1-3. The fourth state machine prevents the NuBus from indefinitely awaiting an acknowledge, by generating an **acknowledge cycle** in response to /START after 256 bus cycles (25.6 microseconds). A wait this long occurs when the processor makes an access to nonfunctional addresses, perhaps because the card being addressed is not present in any of the NuBus slots.

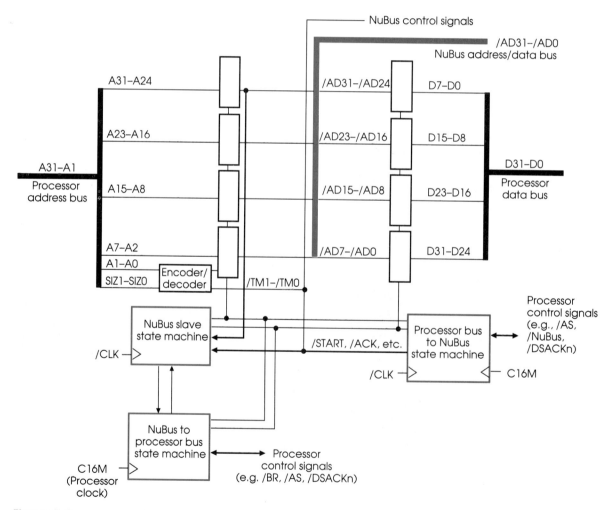

Figure 1-3
Bus interface unit (BIU) architecture

Processor bus to NuBus state machine

The processor bus to NuBus state machine (see Figure 1-3) is activated whenever the MC68020 processor generates a physical address from $6000 0000 through $FFFF FFFF in the data or program address spaces (see the access space map, Figure 1-4). The state machine synchronizes the request with the NuBus clock and presents the same address over the NuBus. If a slave device on NuBus responds, the data is transferred. If no slave responds, a NuBus timeout occurs and a bus error (/BERR) is sent to the processor. The processor can then determine the cause of the error.

❖ *Note:* A special check is made for access to $F0xx xxxx, which is the main logic board's slot address; if attempted, a bus error (/BERR) is generated immediately and no NuBus transaction is attempted.

NuBus to processor bus state machines

A NuBus to processor bus data transfer is controlled by two state machines (see Figure 1-3).

The NuBus to processor bus state machine controls accesses from the NuBus, through the processor bus, to RAM, ROM, and I/O. For example, if an address from $0000 0000 through $3FFF FFFF is presented on NuBus, then the NuBus to processor bus state machine requests the processor bus from the 68020 and performs a RAM access to the same address. Similarly, if an access in address space $F080 0000 through $F0FF FFFF is made on the NuBus, an access in $4x80 0000 through $4xFF FFFF on the processor bus is made to the ROM (see the map in Figure 1-4). Chapter 4 provides much more detailed information on memory access. See Table 4-2, in particular.

Warning

The ability to access processor bus I/O devices is not intended for normal use. Access to anything other than ROM or RAM will likely not be supported on future systems.

Aliasing occurs when a memory location can be accessed from several different addresses. This usually occurs in computer systems when an incomplete address decoding mechanism is used. For example, on the Macintosh II there are only 256K of ROM; this many locations require only 18 bits of addressing to specify a ROM location. The hardware decode logic interprets any physical address whose upper four address bits (A31–A28) are equal to $4 as a ROM access. So there are 32 minus 4, or 28, bits available to access the locations in a ROM that requires only 18 bits of addressing. This means that 10 address bits are "don't cares" and that on the map of physical addresses there are $2^{10} = 1024$ different addresses (aliases) that will access the same ROM location.

The NuBus to processor bus state machine also monitors and records when the NuBus master initiates an attention-resource-lock cycle, and controls the subsequent events of a resource locked transaction as described in the section "Bus Locking" in Chapter 5.

The NuBus slave state machine is synchronous to the NuBus and tracks the state changes on the NuBus.

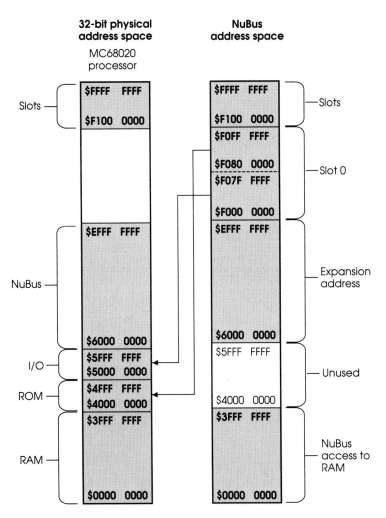

Figure 1-4
Processor bus versus NuBus access addresses

Chapter 2

NuBus Overview

Chapter 2 describes NuBus features, provides a simplified diagram of the NuBus hardware, defines many NuBus terms, classifies the signals used to implement communication over the bus, and discusses the most basic timing and transaction cycle relationships.

NuBus features

The NuBus is used for expansion of the Macintosh II beyond the capabilities of the ports (connectors) on the back of the machine.

NuBus is a 32-bit wide bus chosen by Apple to mechanize the multi-slot expansion of the Macintosh. Table 2-1 shows the highest-level design objectives and the supporting features of the NuBus. Apple chose the NuBus over competitors because it offered cost-effective high performance along with maturity of hardware design and production.

Table 2-1
Design objectives and features

Design objective	Supporting features
System architecture independent	Optimized for 32-bit transfers, but supports 8-bit and 16-bit nonjustified transfers
	Not based on the control structure of a particular microprocessor
High data transfer speed	Clock cycled at a 10 MHz rate (block transfers available but not implemented in the Macintosh II)
Simplicity of protocol	Reads and writes are the only operations used
	I/O and interrupts are memory mapped
	Single, large physical address space allows all addressable cards or other resources to be uniformly accessed
Small pin count	Multiplexed data or address lines
	Simplified connection, only 51 signals plus power and ground lines
Ease of system configuration	Geographical addressing (ID lines) enables interface system to be free of DIP switches and jumpers
	Distributed, parallel arbitration eliminates jumper wiring of slots with missing cards (daisy chaining)

NuBus elements

The NuBus is a synchronous bus; all transitions and signal samplings are synchronized to a central system clock. However, it has many of the features of an asynchronous bus; transactions may be a variable number of clock periods long. This design provides the adaptability of an asynchronous bus with the design simplicity of a synchronous bus.

Figure 2-1 is a simplified representation of a typical NuBus system. In addition to the slot identification (ID), clock, address/data, and arbitration lines shown in the diagram, there are system reset, parity, power fail warning, non-master request, and data transfer control lines.

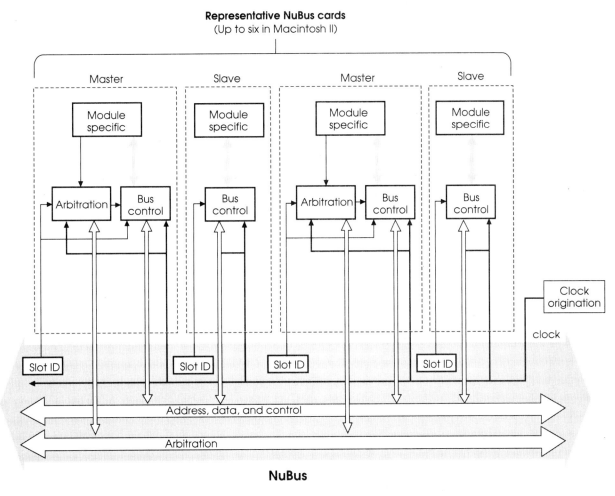

Figure 2-1
Simplified NuBus diagram

NuBus supports only read and write operations in a single address space, in contrast to some other bus designs. I/O and interrupts may be accomplished within these read and write mechanisms. In the Macintosh II, however, interrupts are detected through the /NMRQ line (see "Interrupt Operations" in Chapter 3).

The cards in NuBus slots are peers; no card or slot is a default master. The exception is that only one card drives the system clock line; the clock is supplied by the Macintosh II main logic board. Each slot has an ID code hard-wired into the main logic board of the Macintosh II. This allows cards to differentiate themselves without the computer user having to arrange jumpers or adjust DIP switches.

The NuBus supports multiprocessing and other sophisticated system architectures with a few simple mechanisms explained in Chapter 3.

NuBus signal classifications

NuBus signals can be grouped into six classes based on the functions that they perform. There are also power and ground lines. Table 2-2 shows the NuBus signal classifications.

Table 2-2
Classes of NuBus signals

Classification	Signal	Signal description	Number of pins
Utility	/RESET	Reset	1
	/CLK	Clock	1
	/PFW	Power fail warning	1
	/NMRQ	Non-master request	1
Control	/START	Start	1
	/ACK	Acknowledge	1
	/TM0	Transfer mode 0	1
	/TM1	Transfer mode 1	1
Address/data	/AD31–/AD0	Address/data	32
Arbitration	/ARB3–/ARB0	Arbitration	4
	/RQST	Request	1
Parity	/SP	System parity	1
	/SPV	System parity valid	1
Slot ID	/ID3–/ID0	Slot identification	4
		Total signals	**51**
Power/ground	+5V		11
	+12V		2
	–12V		2
	–5.2V (not supplied) †		8
	GND	Ground	22
		Total pin count	**96**

† These pins are wired together but not supplied with power from the Macintosh II.

NuBus timing

The NuBus system clock has a 100 nanosecond (ns) period with a 75 ns high, 25 ns low duty cycle. Figure 2-2 shows the basic timing for most NuBus signals. The low to high transition of /CLK is used to drive and release signals on the bus. Signals are sampled on the high to low transition of the clock. The asymmetric duty cycle of the clock provides 75 ns for propagation and setup time. Bus skew problems are avoided by having 25 ns between the sample and drive edges.

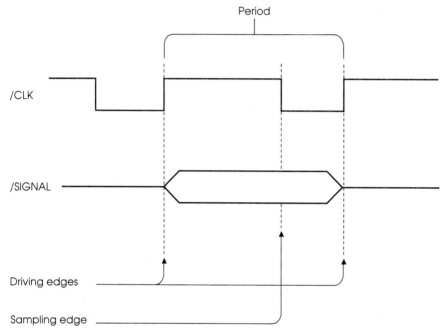

Figure 2-2
NuBus signal timing

Definitions

Table 2-3 defines terms used throughout Part I and applicable to Macintosh II and its
NuBus expansion interface. The relationships among some of these terms are
illustrated in Figures 2-2 and 2-3. All NuBus signals are active (asserted) when low; a
slash preceding a signal name indicates that it is active-low: /SIGNALNAME (for
example, /START).

Table 2-3
Basic definitions

Term	Definition
Acknowledge (ack) cycle	Last period of a transaction during which /ACK is asserted by a slave responding to a master. See Figure 2-3.
Arbitration contest	The mechanism used to choose which of two or more cards requesting control of the bus will become the next bus master. The arbitration contest requires two bus periods (at 100 ns each).
Asserted	The logic state of an active-low signal line when the line is driven low. All NuBus signal lines are active-low.
Attention cycle	The name given to a particular kind of start cycle, one in which both /START and /ACK are asserted. There are two types, attention-null and attention-resource-lock cycles. See "Resource Locking" in Chapter 5.
Attention-null cycle	A type of attention cycle.
Bus lock	A mechanism for providing continuing tenure (bus ownership) by a single card. The extended tenure may include multiple transactions or attention cycles. One type of attention cycle is an attention-resource-lock (often shortened to "resource lock"); therefore a bus lock may or may not include a resource lock.
Card	A printed circuit board or card connected to the bus in parallel with other cards. Also called a device or a module.
Cycle	One period of the NuBus clock, nominally 100 ns in duration and beginning at the rising edge. See Figure 2-2.

(continued)

Table 2-3 (continued)
Basic definitions

Term	Definition
Data cycle	Any period in which data is known to be valid and acknowledged. It includes acknowledge cycles, as well as intermediate data cycles within a block transfer. (Block data transfer is not implemented in the Macintosh II.) See Figure 2-3.
Drive	The action of a card when it causes a bus signal line to be in a known, determinate state.
Driving edge	The rising edge (low to high) of the central system clock (/CLK). See Figure 2-2.
High	For an active-low signal, synonymous with inactive, deasserted, unasserted, false, and released.
Inactive	For an active-low signal, synonymous with high.
Low	For an active-low signal, synonymous with active and asserted.
Master	A card that initiates the addressing of another card or the processor on the main logic board. The card addressed is at that time acting as a slave.
Open collector	A bus driver that drives a line low or doesn't drive it at all.
Parked	The condition when a bus master has completed a transaction and released /RQST, and before any other card has asserted /RQST. Referred to as bus parking, discussed in Chapter 5.
Period	The 100 ns period of /CLK (shown in Figure 2-2) consisting of a 75 ns high state and a 25 ns low state.
Released	For an active-low signal, synonymous with high, inactive, deasserted, unasserted, and false.
Sampling edge	The falling edge (high to low) of the central system clock (/CLK). See Figure 2-2.
Slave	A card that responds to being addressed by another card acting as a master. The Macintosh II main logic board is a card which may be either master or slave. Some cards may be slave-only in function because they lack the circuitry to arbitrate in a bus ownership contest.

Table 2-3 (continued)
Basic definitions

Term	Definition
Slot	A connector attached to the bus. A card may be inserted into any of the slots when more than one is provided (Macintosh II provides six slots).
Slot ID	The hex number ($9 through $E in the Macintosh II) corresponding to each card slot. Each slot ID is established by the main logic board of the Macintosh II and communicated to the card through the /IDx lines.
Slot space	The upper one sixteenth of the total address space. These addresses are in the form $Fsxx xxxx where F, s, and x are hex digits of 4 bits each. This address space is geographically divided among the NuBus slots according to slot ID number (s).
Start cycle	The first period of a transaction during which /START is asserted. See Figure 2-3. The start cycle is one bus clock period long; the transfer mode and the address are valid during this cycle.
Super slot space	The large portion of memory in the range $9000 0000 through $EFFF FFFF. NuBus addresses of the form $sxxx xxxx (that is, $s000 0000 through $sFFF FFFF) reference the super slot space that is assigned to the card in slot s, where s is an ID digit in the range $9 through $E.
Tenure	A time period of unbroken bus ownership by a single master. A master may lock the bus and, during one tenure, perform several transactions. The concept of bus locking is further explained in Chapter 5 in a section titled "Locking."
Transaction	A transaction is a complete NuBus operation such as read or write. In the Macintosh II, a transaction is made up of a start cycle, wait cycles as required by the responding card, and an acknowledge cycle. Start cycles are one clock period long and convey address and command information. Acknowledge cycles are also one clock period long and convey data and acknowledgement information. See Figure 2-3.

(continued)

Table 2-3 (continued)
Basic definitions

Term	Definition
Three-state	A bus driver that drives a line low or high or doesn't drive it at all. Also commonly called *tri-state*.
Unasserted	For an active-low signal, synonymous with high, deasserted, false, inactive, and released.
Word	In Part I, *word* refers to a NuBus word and is 32 bits long and a halfword is 16 bits (usage consistent with the Texas Instruments NuBus specification). Chapter 8, "NuBus Card Firmware" uses data types byte, word, and long in Table 8-1; this inconsistency results from the bridge between 16- and 32-bit microprocessors. As used in Part II of this book, *word* refers to an SE-Bus or MC68000 word and is 16 bits long.

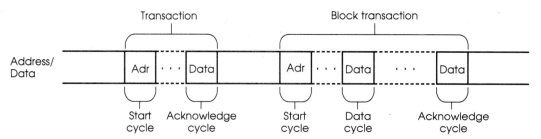

Figure 2-3
Cycle and transaction relationships

Chapter 3

NuBus Data Transfer

After describing the utility signals, this chapter focuses on the process of transferring data over the NuBus interface from a master to a slave. Chapter 5 discusses how the bus master is selected from the several cards competing for the bus, and how all the other cards desiring service are accommodated.

Utility signals

This section identifies the signal lines which serve utility functions for the NuBus interface. The Macintosh II main logic board provides the structure and the slot connectors; it also provides the clock and reset signal sources and bus timeout circuitry.

Clock signal

Clock (/CLK), driven from a single source, synchronizes bus arbitration and data transfers between system cards. /CLK has an asymmetric duty-cycle of 75% high and a constant nominal frequency of 10 MHz. In general, signals are changed at the rising (driving) edge of /CLK, and they are sampled at the falling (sampling) edge.

Reset signal

Reset (/RESET) is an open-collector line that is asserted asynchronously to the NuBus clock. When asserted for a single clock period, /RESET causes a NuBus interface initialization for all cards (bus reset).

The Macintosh II asserts /RESET at initial power-up, when the Reset button is pressed, or when the MC68020 executes a reset instruction. /RESET stays asserted at least 200 milliseconds when not generated by the MC68020.

Card slot identification signals

Identification signals 0 through 3 (/ID3–/ID0) are binary coded to specify the physical location of each card. The highest numbered slot ($F) has the four signals wired low. The lowest numbered slot ($0) has all ID signals open. In the Macintosh II there are six slots numbered $9 through $E. The Macintosh II main logic board is addressed as slot $0.

The distributed arbitration logic uses the ID numbers to uniquely identify cards for arbitration contests. See Chapter 5, "NuBus Arbitration."

The ID signals are also used to allocate a small portion of the total address space to each card. The upper 1/16th (256 MB) of the entire 4 gigabyte NuBus address space is called **slot space.** If /ID3–/ID0 are used to specify NuBus address lines /AD27–/AD24, each of the 16 possible NuBus card slots has an address of the form $Fsxx xxxx, where s is the 4-bit hex digit for a particular slot. This address range allocates 16 MB of address space (1/16th of 256 MB) per NuBus card slot, an address region called a **slot.**

However, by using the /ID3–/ID0 bits in a different way, a second natural address decode of what is called **super slot space** can be easily performed. If /ID3–/ID0 are used to specify NuBus address lines /AD31–/AD28, each of the 16 possible NuBus card slots has an address of the form $sxxx xxxx, where s is the 4-bit hex digit for a particular slot. This address range allocates 256 MB of address space (1/16th of 4 GB) per NuBus card slot, an address region called a **super slot.** Thus each physical slot has allocated to it a slot space and a super slot space.

This fixed address allocation, based solely on the slot location of a card, enables the design of systems that are free of jumpers and switches. Chapter 4, "Access to Address Space," discusses memory addressing in detail.

Power fail warning

Power fail warning (/PFW) may be asserted asynchronous with respect to the driving edge of /CLK and indicates that the power is about to fail. In the Macintosh II this signal is also used to control the power supply. Driving /PFW high will turn the computer on; driving /PFW low will turn it off.

See Chapter 6, "NuBus Card Electrical Design Guide," for /PFW drive requirements in case a card is to control the power supply through the NuBus.

Non-master request

Non-master request (/NMRQ) is a signal asynchronous to /CLK that provides an interrupt mechanism for cards that are intended to be slave-only. Such cards avoid the cost of implementing arbitration logic.

Signal line determinacy

The bus driving circuitry, the bus transmission line parameters, and the terminating impedances must be coordinated to make the signal lines determinate within the specified setup and hold times of the NuBus clock.

A signal line is determinate by virtue of satisfying one of the following conditions:

☐ If a signal is driven during clock cycle n, then it is determinate during cycle n.

☐ If a signal is unasserted during cycle n, and is not driven during cycle n + 1, then that signal is guaranteed to remain unasserted during cycle n + 1.

☐ If an open collector signal is driven asserted during cycle n and is not driven during cycle n + 1, then it is guaranteed to be unasserted during cycle n + 1.

☐ If a three-state signal is asserted during cycle n, and is not driven during cycles n + 1 and n + 2, then it is *not* guaranteed determinate during cycle n + 1, but the line is guaranteed to be unasserted during cycle n + 2.

Data transfer signals

The bus data transfer signals, including control, address/data, and bus parity, are all three-state.

Control signals

This section describes the primary functions of the four NuBus control signals.

Transfer start (/START) is driven for only one clock period by the current bus master at the beginning of a transaction. /START indicates to the slaves that the address/data signals are carrying a valid address.

Transfer acknowledge (/ACK) is driven for only one clock period by the addressed slave device and indicates the completion of the transaction. An exception to the foregoing is attention cycles, when the bus master asserts both /START and /ACK. See "Attention Cycle Operation" later in this chapter.

Transfer mode 0 and 1 (/TM0, /TM1) are driven by the current bus master during start cycles to indicate the type of bus operation being initiated. They are also driven by bus slaves during acknowledge cycles to denote the type of acknowledgement. /TM0 and /TM1 encoding for start cycles is given in Table 3-1.

Address/data signals

Address/data 0 through 31 (/AD31–/AD0) signals are multiplexed to carry a 32-bit byte address at the beginning of each transaction and up to 32 bits of data later in the transaction. Note that the /AD0 and /AD1 signals, along with /TM0 and /TM1, carry transfer mode information during the start cycle. This transfer mode encoding is shown in Table 3-1.

Bus parity signals

System parity (/SP) transmits parity information between NuBus cards that implement NuBus parity checking. Future Apple products may employ this feature, but the Macintosh II does not provide parity checking, so this line is pulled high.

System parity valid (/SPV) indicates that the /SP bit is being used. Cards that do not generate bus parity will never drive /SPV active and cards that do not check parity will ignore /SP and /SPV. Future Apple products may employ this feature, but in the Macintosh II this line is pulled high.

Data transfer specifications

The NuBus supports reads and writes of several different data sizes. Although optimized for transactions of words and blocks of words, the NuBus also supports byte and halfword transactions. The base unit of addressability is a NuBus word; /AD31–/AD2 specify the appropriate word. The two least significant address bits (/AD1–/AD0), along with /TM1–/TM0, specify the transfer mode; that mode determines which part of the addressed word is to be transferred, as shown in Table 3-1.

Table 3-1
Transfer mode coding

/TM1	/TM0	/AD1	/AD0	Type of cycle
L	L	L	L	Write byte 3
L	L	L	H	Write byte 2
L	L	H	L	Write byte 1
L	L	H	H	Write byte 0
L	H	L	L	Write halfword 1
L	H	L	H	Write block
L	H	H	L	Write halfword 0
L	H	H	H	Write word
H	L	L	L	Read byte 3
H	L	L	H	Read byte 2
H	L	H	L	Read byte 1
H	L	H	H	Read byte 0
H	H	L	L	Read halfword 1
H	H	L	H	Read block
H	H	H	L	Read halfword 0
H	H	H	H	Read word

Bit 31   Bit 0

NuBus word			
Halfword 1		Halfword 0	
Byte 3	Byte 2	Byte 1	Byte 0

Figure 3-1
Layout of words, halfwords, and bytes

All NuBus data transfers are unjustified as shown in Figure 3-1. A byte of data is conveyed on the same signal lines regardless of the transfer mode used to access it. Therefore, bytes with address 0 **modulo** 4 are always carried by /AD0 through /AD7, bytes 1 modulo 4 by /AD8 through /AD15, bytes 2 modulo 4 by /AD16 through /AD23, bytes 3 modulo 4 by /AD24 through /AD31. This unjustified data path approach allows straightforward connection of 8-bit, 16-bit, and 32-bit devices.

Single data cycle transactions

The simplest transactions on the NuBus convey one data item and consist of a start cycle and a subsequent acknowledge cycle. These transactions are either reads or writes of bytes, halfwords, or words.

All transactions are initiated by a bus master which drives /START active while driving the /TMx, /AD0, and /AD1 signals to define the cycle type. The remaining /ADx signals are also driven to convey the address. The transaction is completed when the responding slave drives /ACK active while driving status information on the /TMx lines. For write transactions, the master must switch the /ADx lines from address to data information in the second clock period and hold that data until acknowledged. In read cycles, the slave drives the data simultaneously with the acknowledge cycle in the last period.

The following abbrevations are used in the timing diagrams and step sequences in this section:

R   Rising edge of /CLK
F   Falling edge of /CLK

Read transactions

Figure 3-2 shows the timing for read bus transactions other than block transfers. Block transfers are not supported in the Macintosh II, but they may be used in future products. Read operations with data widths of 8, 16, and 32 bits are selected by the transfer mode signals (/TMx) and the two low-order address signals (/AD1 and /AD0) as shown in Table 3-1. The slave must put the requested data item on either 8, 16, or all 32 of the /AD31 through /AD0 signals. Any bits other than the requested data may be driven either high or low by the slave; they must be determinate.

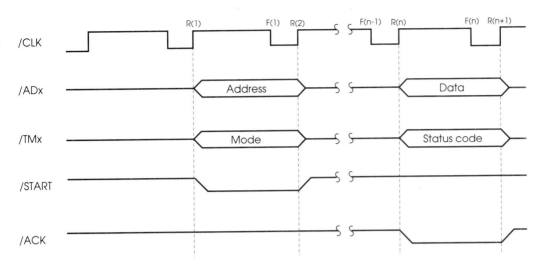

Figure 3-2
Timing of NuBus read transaction

Once the bus master has acquired the bus, a read bus transaction involves the
following steps:

R(1)[†]   The bus master asserts /START and the appropriate /ADx and /TMx
            lines to initiate the transfer.

F(1)[‡]   The bus slaves sample the /ADx and /TMx lines.

R(2)   The bus master releases the /ADx, /TMx, and /START lines and waits for
            /ACK.

R(n)[§]   The bus slave places the requested data onto the /ADx lines, asserts
            /ACK, and places the appropriate status code on /TM0 and /TM1.

F(n)   The bus master samples the /ADx and /TMx lines to receive the data and
            note any error condition.

R(n + 1)   The bus slave releases the /ADx and /ACK lines and /TMx lines. This
            may be the R(1) of the next transaction.

[†] R is the rising edge of /CLK.
[‡] F is the falling edge of /CLK.
[§] $2 \leq n < 256$, the system defined timeout period.

Write transactions

Figure 3-3 shows the timing for write operations other than block transfers. Block transfers are not supported in the Macintosh II, but they may be used in future products. Write operations with data widths of 8, 16, and 32 bits are selected by the transfer mode signals (/TMx) and the two low-order address bits (/AD1 and /AD0).

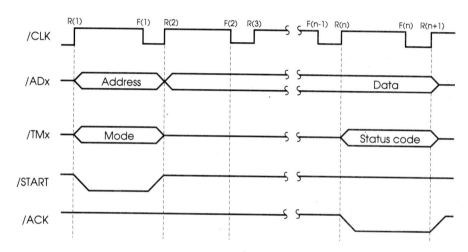

Figure 3-3
Timing of NuBus write transaction

The bus master has the responsibility for aligning data onto the appropriate /ADx lines for halfword and byte writes. For example, a write of byte 3 requires that the data be placed on /AD24 through /AD31; all other /ADx lines are not defined and are driven to either a high or low state. (See Table 3-1 and Figure 4-2.)

Once the bus master has acquired the bus, a write bus transaction involves the following steps:

R(1)[†]   The bus master asserts /START and the appropriate /ADx and /TMx lines to initiate the transfer.

F(1)[‡]   The bus slave samples the /ADx and /TMx lines.

R(2)   The bus master places the data to be written onto the /ADx lines, releases the /START and /TMx lines, and waits for /ACK.

F(2)–F(n)[§]   The bus slave samples the /ADx lines to capture the data. The data may be sampled before or during the assertion of /ACK.

R(n)   The bus slave asserts /ACK and places the appropriate status code on /TM0 and /TM1 when the data is accepted.

F(n)   The bus master samples /ACK and /TMx to determine end of transaction.

R(n + 1)   The bus master releases the /ADx lines while the bus slave releases the /ACK and /TMx lines.

[†] R is the rising edge of /CLK.
[‡] F is the falling edge of /CLK.
[§] $2 \leq n < 256$, the system defined timeout period.

Acknowledgement

During acknowledge cycles the addressed slave drives the /TMx lines while it drives /ACK. The /TMx lines provide status information to the current bus master as shown in Table 3-2.

Table 3-2
Status information coding

/TM1	/TM0	Type of acknowledge
L	L	Bus transfer complete
L	H	Error
H	L	Bus timeout error
H	H	Try again later

Bus transfer complete: The bus transfer complete response indicates the normal valid completion of a bus transaction.

Error: During a read or write operation, certain error conditions may occur. The transaction terminates in a normal manner and the bus master has the responsibility for handling the error condition reported.

Bus timeout: If an unimplemented address location is accessed, or for any other reason a slave does not respond to a start cycle address, the attempted transaction is acknowledged with a bus timeout error response. This timeout response indicates that the system defined timeout period has elapsed while the bus is busy (that is, the bus is between start and acknowledge cycles) and no data transfer acknowledge has occurred. Bus timeout support logic on the Macintosh II main logic board enforces a period of 256 clock periods, or 25.6 microseconds, and assumes the role of the non-responding slave; it generates an acknowledge cycle with a bus timeout error code.

Try again later: This response status code indicates that a slave is unable to respond at this time to a data transfer request from a bus master. The master should retry the transaction, and slaves should be designed so that a large number of retries are not required.

On the Macintosh II, a NuBus access by the MC68020 that terminates with a try again later, error, or bus timeout response generates a bus error exception.

Attention cycle operation

An attention cycle is defined as a bus cycle during which both /START and /ACK are asserted. During an attention cycle the /TMx lines have a different function. Two of the four available codings are used at present, as shown in Table 3-3.

Table 3-3
Attention cycle coding

/TM1	/TM0	Type of attention cycle
L	L	Attention-null
L	H	Reserved
H	L	Attention-resource-lock
H	H	Reserved

During an attention cycle, the /ADx lines are ignored by all bus cards and no data may be transferred.

Attention cycles are used to reinitiate bus arbitration (attention-null) or to signal a resource lock (attention-resource-lock), or both. Refer to Chapter 5, "NuBus Arbitration," for a detailed explanation of bus arbitration and resource locking.

Attention-null: The attention-null cycle has two uses:

☐ to re-initiate arbitration after the bus has been requested and won, but the new bus owner decides not to transfer data (in this case, the new bus owner must generate an attention-null cycle)

☐ to indicate the end of a data transfer using a locked resource

Attention-resource-lock: /TM1 high (H) and /TM0 low (L) signal an attention-resource-lock cycle at the beginning of a sequence of locked transactions constituting a locked tenure of the current bus master. During this tenure, cards with lockable multi-port resources lock them against access by local processors other than the NuBus master. That tenure is terminated by an attention-null cycle.

Implementation rules: The following rules should be observed:

☐ Masters must drive /ACK high during their start cycle to guarantee that /ACK is in the unasserted state and the start cycle is not interpreted as an attention cycle.

☐ Masters must ensure that the first /ACK terminates a transaction. An attention cycle immediately following the acknowledge cycle *must not* latch data.

☐ Slaves must qualify /START with the logical complement of /ACK to decode a start cycle. Otherwise, an attention cycle could be misinterpreted as a start cycle.

Interrupt operations

Three possible ways to handle NuBus interrupts are available, but only one way is used by the Macintosh II.

By write transaction

Interrupts on the NuBus can be implemented as write transactions. *Interrupts are not done this way on the Macintosh II.* Interrupt operations require no unique signals or protocols. Any card on the NuBus that is capable of becoming bus master can interrupt a processor card by performing a write operation into an area of memory that is monitored by that processor. Any address range on the processor card can be defined as its interrupt space. This allows interrupts to be posted to individual processors and allows interrupt priority to be software specified by memory mapping the priority level.

By slots sharing a single NuBus line (/NMRQ)

The individual slot /NMRQ (non-master request) signals may drive a single NuBus line (/NMRQ), in which case, the system processor will have available only the wired-OR of all of the slot /NMRQ signals. In this case, the software must poll the slots capable of generating the bus /NMRQ signal to determine the source or sources of the interrupt.

By dedicated /NMRQ line from each slot (Macintosh II)

The Macintosh II uses a separate (non-NuBus) line (/NMRQ) from each slot to support interrupts (see Figure 1-1).

Each card slot has a unique /NMRQ line driving an OR gate whose output is a real hardware interrupt signal to the MC68020 (through VIA2). In addition, each of the /NMRQ lines are independently pollable by the processor, to allow the software to communicate with the appropriate handlers for each of the cards asserting /NMRQ.

Block data transfers

Block transfers are not implemented in the Macintosh II, but they may be implemented in future Apple products. The following is for completeness in describing the NuBus.

Block transfers are transactions which consist of a start cycle, multiple data cycles from or to sequential address locations, and an acknowledge cycle. The number of data cycles is controlled by the master and communicated during the start cycle. Allowed lengths of block transfers are 2, 4, 8, and 16 words. (Only 32-bit NuBus word transfers are supported in block mode.)

The /TM1, /TM0, /AD1, /AD0 encoding for block transfers is shown in Table 3-1. The starting address of the block must correspond to the size of the block and is encoded by the /AD2 through /AD5 lines as shown in Table 3-4.

During block transfers, each data cycle is acknowledged by the responding slave. The intermediate acknowledges are data cycles where /TM0 is active and /TM1 and /ACK are both inactive. For intermediate acknowledgements, /TM0 has the same significance and timing as the /ACK signal for nonblock transfers. The acknowledgement of the final word transfer is a standard acknowledge cycle. Status codes are shown in Table 3-2.

Table 3-4
Block size and starting address coding

/AD5	/AD4	/AD3	/AD2	Block size (words)	Block starting address
X	X	X	H	2	(AD31–AD3)000
X	X	H	L	4	(AD31–AD4)0000
X	H	L	L	8	(AD31–AD5)00000
H	L	L	L	16	(AD31–AD6)000000
L	L	L	L	Error	

Block read

Figure 3-4 shows the timing for a NuBus block read transaction. See Table 3-1 for the /TM1, /TM0, /AD1, /AD0 encoding which initiates block reads. The /AD5 through /AD2 lines determine the size and starting address of the transaction as shown in Table 3-4. The responding slave drives data onto the bus and the initiating bus master accepts the data on each intermediate or final acknowledge. Assertion of /TM0 is used by the responding slave as an intermediate acknowledge, meaning that the next consecutive word of data is ready to be put on the bus.

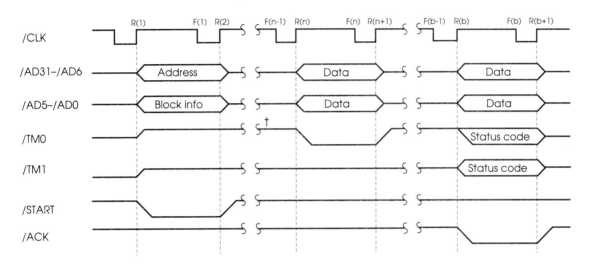

† The addressed slave is responsible for driving /TM0 to the desired state between R(n) and R(b+1).

Figure 3-4
Timing of NuBus block read transaction

Once the bus master has acquired the bus, a block read consists of these steps:

R(1)†   The bus master asserts /START and the appropriate /ADx and /TMx lines to initiate the transfer.

F(1)‡   The bus slaves sample the /ADx and /TMx lines.

R(2)   The bus master releases the /ADx, /TMx, and /START lines and waits for an intermediate acknowledge (/TM0 asserted).

R(n)§   The bus slave places the first word of requested data on the /ADx lines and asserts /TM0.

F(n)   The bus master samples the /ADx lines and /TM0 to capture data. /TM0 is asserted and data is next data item.

R(n + 1)   If the next consecutive word of data is not ready to be put on the bus, the slave drives /TM0 unasserted until the word is ready.

The previous three steps are repeated for ascending addresses until B − 1 words have been transferred, where B is the block size (2, 4, 8, or 16).

R(b)¶   The bus slave places the final word of requested data onto the /ADx lines, asserts /ACK, and places the appropriate status code on /TM0 and /TM1.

F(b)   The bus master samples the /ADx and /TMx lines to receive the data and note any error conditions.

R(b + 1)   The bus slave releases the /ADx, /ACK, and /TMx lines.

† R is the rising edge of /CLK.
‡ F is the falling edge of /CLK.
§ 2 ≤ n ≤ 256, the system defined timeout period.
¶ 2 ≤ b ≤ 256B.

Block write

Figure 3-5 is a timing diagram for a NuBus block write operation. Block writes are similar to block reads except the bus master drives the data bus while the slave accepts data. The format for describing block size and starting address is the same as for block reads.

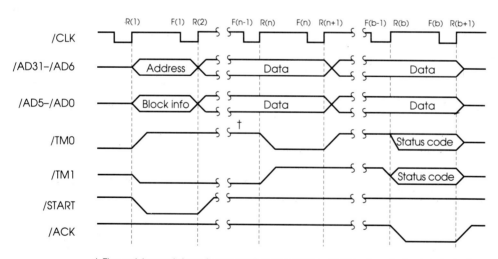

† The addressed slave is responsible for driving /TM0 to the desired state between R(n) and R(b+1).

Figure 3-5
Timing for NuBus block write transaction

Once the bus master has acquired the bus, a block write consists of these steps:

R(1)[†]   The bus master asserts /START and the appropriate /ADx and /TMx lines to initiate the transfer.

F(1)[‡]   The bus slaves sample the /ADx and /TMx lines.

R(2)   The bus master places the data to be written onto the /ADx lines, releases the /START and /TMx lines, and waits for an intermediate acknowledge (/TM0 asserted).

R(n)[§]   The bus slave asserts /TM0 when the first word of data is accepted.

F(n–)   The bus slave samples the /ADx lines to capture the data being written. The n– notation implies the data may be sampled before or during the assertion of /TM0.

R(n + 1)   The bus master places the next consecutive word of data on the bus.

The previous three steps are repeated for ascending addresses until B – 1 words have been transferred, where B is the block size.

R(b)[¶]   The bus slave asserts /ACK and places the appropriate status code on /TM0 and /TM1 when the final word of data is accepted.

F(b–)   The bus slave samples the /ADx lines to capture the data. The b– notation implies the data may be sampled before or during the assertion of /ACK.

R(b + 1)   The bus master releases the /ADx lines while the bus slave releases the /ACK and /TMx lines.

[†] R is the rising edge of /CLK.
[‡] F is the falling edge of /CLK.
[§] $2 \le n \le 256$, the system defined timeout period.
[¶] $2 \le b \le 256B$.

Block transfer errors

Although the length of a block transfer is dictated by the master during the start cycle, a block transfer may be cut short by an error acknowledgement from the slave at any time. The standard status codes shown in Table 3-2 are used.

The speed of a block transfer is controlled by the slave, therefore a master requesting a block transfer must be capable of transferring data at the speed of the *fastest* slave in the system. This could be one word per NuBus clock cycle (one word per 100 ns.). If the master is incapable of transfers at the speed the slave specifies, an *undetectable* overrun (or underrun) occurs.

It is a NuBus specification that if a slave supports any block transfer, it must support all types (byte, halfword, and word). In the case of a block transfer request to a slave that cannot support block transfers, that slave should terminate the first transfer with /ACK and a normal status code. This is *not* considered an error condition. The data should be ignored for read or write purposes.

Non-aligned MC68020 accesses

The MC68020 bus interface allows accesses that do not fall into natural NuBus transactions. For example, a MC68020 program can request a read of a longword at an odd numbered location. This can not be performed in a single NuBus transaction, since it falls across word boundaries.

The Macintosh II to NuBus interface always translates aligned requests into their counterpart on NuBus. However, that interface also provides support for all non-aligned MC68020 accesses (by using the dynamic bus sizing facilities of the MC68020). The Macintosh II to NuBus interface will respond to off-boundary MC68020 requests with DSACKs which tell the processor that the bus is only 16 bits wide. This will cause the MC68020 to make several cycles to fulfill the original request, using an incremented address and decremented size. For each subsequent cycle, the NuBus interface generates an appropriate transaction until the entire request is complete.

Non-aligned reads

Non-aligned reads are mapped into NuBus word (32-bit) reads. This provides the required data in the fewest NuBus transactions. Notice that some non-aligned requests will generate two NuBus cycles. For example, a longword read of $Fs00 0001 generates a word read to $Fs00 0000 and a byte read to $Fs00 0004. The "extra" data provided by the word read is ignored. The reason for the second read being a byte read instead of another word read is that the MC68020 asks for one byte to $FS00 0004, which is a natural NuBus transaction.

Non-aligned writes

Non-aligned writes are supported by breaking the MC68020 request into pieces that can be executed by the NuBus. For example, a longword write to $Fs00 0001 would be performed in three pieces: a byte write to $Fs00 0001, a halfword write to $Fs00 0002, and a byte write to $Fs00 0004.

Data caching

Future systems may implement **data caching** (based upon the MC68030, for example). To support this, RAM-like cards should always supply all 32 bits, regardless of the NuBus request. For example, if a NuBus request is presented for a byte, the card should present data for all four bytes in the NuBus word.

Note that the caching of data can be controlled by software; that is, some address spaces can be declared as non-cacheable. Any card that is not capable of supporting a full 32-bit read must have its corresponding driver software set up the caching control appropriately.

A similar caveat concerns the non-aligned cases. If a card cannot support a full 32-bit read, the software must ensure that only appropriately aligned and sized operations are requested.

Compliance categories

Various categories of cards may be designed that conform to the NuBus specification, but do not support all NuBus features. Masters and slaves do not need to support all transfer types. Any combination of 8-, 16-, and 32-bit single data transfers, with the card acting as either master or slave, is allowable. Masters need not support all possible block transfers. However, slaves must support all block transfer lengths if they support block transfer at all.

The decisions about how non-aligned accesses work and the rules for data caching have been made to provide the highest performance for 32-bit wide cards. These cards may have all the necessary logic and bus tranceivers to support these rules.

Many Apple NuBus slot cards may be dumb. It is not required that all devices respond with an error status code for transfer types that they do not handle; it is acceptable to merely respond with an /ACK assertion.

Such dumb cards must be managed only by device drivers that are designed to communicate with them appropriately. One of the functions of the declaration ROM is to provide indications of the capabilities of the card.

Driver-supported cards are those that are accessed indirectly via a software driver. You can write the driver to manage any idiosyncrasies of the card. For these types of cards, you have relative freedom in the tradeoffs you make in the design of the hardware, because you can write the driver software to accommodate them.

Peer cards are cards that are designed to execute code that is not specialized to the card; for example, two cards that execute cooperating processes to solve a problem. These cards must be more general in their hardware design, because the code that executes on them assumes no restrictions in types of access, size of data operands, and so forth.

In general, peer cards must be designed to support the maximum size of transfer that any of their peers are capable of supporting. In particular, a peer card that is designed to cooperate with the MC68020 of the Macintosh II main logic board must properly handle 32-bit (NuBus word) transfers. If such a card contains, for example, an MC68000 and has a local bus that is naturally 16 bits in width, the card must provide the hardware support in its NuBus interface to handle such 32-bit transfers. This would involve doing two local bus cycles for each NuBus word request.

A card with an MC68000 processor must make two NuBus halfword requests to satisfy an access to a longword quantity (for example, a pointer value). The Macintosh II properly responds to these two requests. The same instruction, when executed by the MC68020 of the Macintosh II main logic board makes one NuBus word request. If the card with the MC68000 does not respond with the correct 32-bit quantity, the program obviously does not execute correctly.

You should clearly indicate in the card's documentation exactly which kind of card it is and what types of accesses it supports.

Memory devices, however, must support all transfer types except for block transfer; the devices should always respond with all 32 bits in the addressed longword (NuBus word). This rule allows RAM cards to be used as if they were on-board RAM in order to support non-aligned transfers, 68020 bit-field instructions, 68030 caching (possible in future products), and so forth.

Chapter 4

Access to
Address Space

This chapter describes how cards connected to the Macintosh II through the NuBus slots can access address space. The discussion is in three sections:

☐ a general description of the NuBus **address space** and how it is accessed in both 24-bit and 32-bit modes

☐ a discussion of how the NuBus address space is allocated, including its mapping of the Macintosh II address space

☐ a description of the bit structure of NuBus messages, and how it differs from the MC68020 bus architecture

In addition to the memory areas it uses for its own operations, every NuBus card must contain a declaration ROM area that is addressable in the slot space of the card. Slot space is defined in the next section. The declaration ROM contains certain standard data structures that are accessed by the Macintosh II Slot Manager. These structures are defined in Chapter 8, "NuBus Card Firmware."

Address space

The NuBus architecture allows full 32-bit addresses, providing four gigabytes of address space. The upper one-sixteenth (256 megabytes) of the NuBus address space is called **slot space.** As shown in Figure 4-1, this addressing region is further divided into 16 regions of 16 megabytes apiece, each of which constitutes the slot space for one possible slot ID. NuBus addresses of the form $Fsxx xxxx (that is, $Fs00 0000 through $FsFF FFFF) reference the slot space that belongs to the card in slot s, where s is an ID digit in the range $9 through $E. Because the Macintosh II uses only slot IDs $9 through $E, however, only the six slot spaces $F9xx xxxx through $FExx xxxx are actually used. This system of fixed address allocations, based solely on a card's slot location, makes it possible for you to design cards that are free of jumpers and configuration switches.

Warning

Whenever possible, use 32-bit addressing conventions and methods. This will be your best guarantee of future software compatibility.

When a Macintosh II card needs to address more than 16 megabytes, it can access an additional region of the NuBus address space. As shown in Figure 4-1, the area from $9000 0000 through $EFFF FFFF is called **super slot space,** and is divided into regions of 256 megabytes each. NuBus addresses of the form $sxxx xxxx (that is, $s000 0000 through $sFFF FFFF) reference the super slot space that belongs to the card in slot s.

Figure 4-1 also shows the card's declaration ROM space, discussed in Chapter 8.

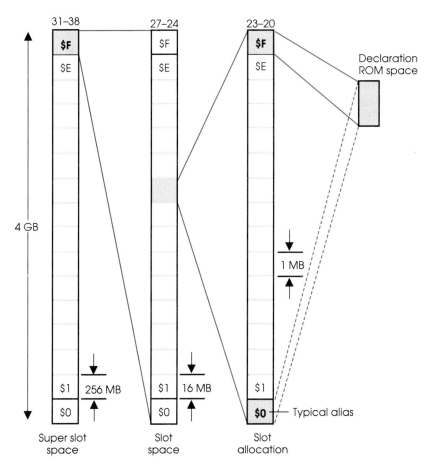

Figure 4-1
NuBus address space

As explained in the chapter "The Operating System Utilities" of *Inside Macintosh,* Volume V, the Macintosh II operates in either 32-bit or 24-bit mode. In 32-bit mode, it can access all the address space in both the slot and super slot spaces of any slot card. In 24-bit mode, it can address only one megabyte of each card's slot space. In 24-bit mode, the Macintosh II hardware translates 24-bit addresses of the form $sx xxxx into 32-bit addresses of the form $Fs0x xxxx, where s is a digit in the range $9 through $E.

Addresses of the form $Fssx xxxx access the same NuBus slot in both 24-bit and 32-bit modes. However, if you use an address of this form in 24-bit mode, the system will translate it into a NuBus address of $Fs0x xxxx. In 32-bit mode it will remain unchanged. Hence if you need less than one megabyte of address space to be accessible from NuBus, you should design your card to use only bits /AD19–/AD0. By ignoring bits /AD23–/AD20, you guarantee that addresses of the form $Fssx xxxx will be valid in both 24-bit and 32-bit modes.

The Macintosh II hardware translates other 24-bit addresses above $7F FFFF into different 32-bit addresses. The full translation algorithm is shown in Table 4-1.

Table 4-1
24-bit to 32-bit address translations

24-bit address range	32-bit address range	Notes
$00 0000–$7F FFFF	$0000 0000–$007F FFFF	
$80 0000–$8F FFFF	$4000 0000–$400F FFFF	
$s0 0000–$sF FFFF	$Fs00 0000–$Fs0F FFFF	s in range $9 through $E
$F0 0000–$FF FFFF	$5000 0000–$500F FFFF	

Macintosh II address allocations

All of the existing Macintosh II address space is accessible from NuBus. It is mapped onto the NuBus address space as shown in Table 4-2.

Table 4-2
NuBus to Macintosh II address mapping

24-bit addresses from MC68020	32-bit addresses from MC68020	NuBus addresses	Used to access Macintosh II system
$xx00 0000 to $xx7F FFFF	$0000 0000 to $007F FFFF	$0000 0000 to $007F FFFF	Present RAM
	$0080 0000 to $3FFF FFFF	$0080 0000 to $3FFF FFFF	Future RAM
$xx80 0000 to $xx8F FFFF	$4000 0000 to $4FFF FFFF	$F080 0000 to $F0FF FFFF	ROM (aliased)
$xxF0 0000 to $xxFF FFFF	$5000 0000 to $5FFF FFFF	$F000 0000 to $F070 FFFF	I/O (aliased); do not access from a slot card
	$6000 0000 to $8FFF FFFF	$6000 0000 to $8FFF FFFF	Presently unused
	$9000 0000 to $EFFF FFFF	$9000 0000 to $EFFF FFFF	Super slot space, slots $9 to $E
$xxF0 0000 to $xxFF FFFF	$F000 0000 to $F0FF FFFF[†]	$F000 0000 to $F0FF FFFF	Slot $0 (Macintosh system)[†]
	$F100 0000 to $F8FF FFFF	$F100 0000 to $F8FF FFFF	Presently unused
$xxs0 0000 to $xxsF FFFF	$Fs00 0000 to $FsFF FFFF or $Fs10 0000 to $FsFF FFFF	$Fs00 0000 to $FsFF FFFF or $Fs10 0000 to $FsFF FFFF	Slot space, slot s (s in the range $9–$E)
	$FF00 0000 to $FFFF FFFF	$FF00 0000 to $FFFF FFFF	Presently unused

[†] If the MC68020 attempts to access addresses in this range, it will immediately generate a bus error (/BERR) exception. No NuBus transaction will take place.

When the MC68020 accesses 32-bit addresses in the range $6000 0000 through $FFFF FFFF (except for $F0xx xxxx), it initiates a NuBus transaction. The mapping shown in Table 4-2 is correct for the Macintosh II. Future Macintosh products may have different mappings.

Slot allocations

In 24-bit mode, the lower one megabyte of each card's slot space is mapped onto a part of the 24-bit Macintosh II address space. This address space is used for communication between the card in that slot and the Macintosh II. For example, NuBus addresses $F900 0000 through $F90F FFFF correspond to 24-bit Macintosh addresses $90 0000 through $9F FFFF and are used by slot $9. All the rest of each slot's NuBus address allocation is available for other uses by the card in that slot and may also be addressed by the Macintosh II system in 32-bit mode and by cards in other slots. These allocations are listed in Table 4-3.

Table 4-3
Slot allocations

Slot	24-bit Macintosh II addresses	NuBus super slot space	NuBus slot space
$9	$90 0000–$9F FFFF	$9000 0000–$9FFF FFFF	$F900 0000–$F9FF FFFF
$A	$A0 0000–$AF FFFF	$A000 0000–$AFFF FFFF	$FA00 0000–$FAFF FFFF
$B	$B0 0000–$BF FFFF	$B000 0000–$BFFF FFFF	$FB00 0000–$FBFF FFFF
$C	$C0 0000–$CF FFFF	$C000 0000–$CFFF FFFF	$FC00 0000–$FCFF FFFF
$D	$D0 0000–$DF FFFF	$D000 0000–$DFFF FFFF	$FD00 0000–$FDFF FFFF
$E	$E0 0000–$EF FFFF	$E000 0000–$EFFF FFFF	$FE00 0000–$FEFF FFFF

Slot $0 corresponds to the Macintosh II itself. It addresses the 16 megabytes of NuBus slot space from $F000 0000 to $F0FF FFFF. It cannot be accessed by the MC68020.

NuBus bit and byte structure

The NuBus bit structure is not the same as the bit structure of the MC68020 bus. For purposes of byte addressing consistency, Apple has chosen to perform **byte swapping** of data between the MC68020 and NuBus. This section explains the rationale and details of this implementation.

As mentioned in Chapter 3, each NuBus addressable byte has a particular byte lane in which it is transferred; all bytes with addresses of the form (xxx modulo 4) = N are transferred in byte lane N. Unfortunately, there is no universal agreement about what the significance of a given addressed byte should be within a larger unit. For example, within a NuBus word, byte 3 is the most significant byte (MSB), while in the 680x0 world, byte 3 is the least significant byte (LSB) of a longword (32-bit) value.

In designing the Macintosh II, a choice had to be made about whether to preserve the significance of bytes between the NuBus and the MC680x0 world or to preserve byte addressing consistency. Note that this choice deals with how the four bytes within a NuBus word and an MC68020 longword are connected to each other.

Apple chose to preserve byte address consistency in the Macintosh II; each of the four bytes of the MC68020 are connected to its corresponding NuBus byte lane. That is, byte *n* of the MC68020 is connected to NuBus byte lane *n*, as shown in Figure 4-2. Notice that bit numbers do not have a direct correspondence between the MC68020 and the NuBus. For example, bits D31–D24 (byte 0) of the MC68020 are connected to bits AD7–AD0 (byte lane 0) of the NuBus.

The significance of a byte within a larger item is reversed in this process. That is, the MSB of a NuBus word is in byte lane 3, while the MSB of a MC68020 longword is in byte 0. Thus, there is an apparent swapping of the bytes between the world of the MC68020 and NuBus; this is referred to as **byte swapping.**

For many cards, byte swapping is not important. However, for cards that interface to processors of different byte ordering, very careful attention must be paid to the NuBus interface. An Intel 80386, for example, has byte ordering identical to NuBus; that is, the LSB of an 80386 word is byte 0, the MSB is byte 3.

Transferring data by *bytes* between such a processor and the NuBus would always produce the correct value. However, when the MC68020 accessed a NuBus *word* from an 80386 on a card, it would read a value whose bytes were swapped in significance. For example, a word read of a location within the 80386 card that contained a 32-bit value of $1234 5678 would be seen as $7856 3412 by the MC68020 because of the byte swapping.

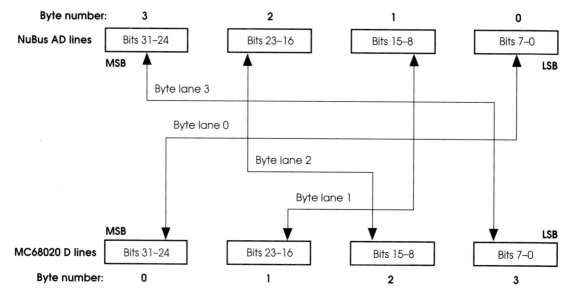

Figure 4-2
Byte lane mapping

The routes by which bytes are transferred between the NuBus and the MC68020 processor are called **byte lanes.** They are numbered to reflect the bytes they carry: that is, byte lane 0 carries byte 0, byte lane 1 carries byte 1, and so on. NuBus encodes the least significant bits in its data word into byte 0 and the most significant bits into byte 3. The MC68020 processor does the reverse: it places its least significant bits in byte 3 and its most significant bits in byte 0. Byte-lane routing is performed automatically by the Macintosh II system. Only the bytes are swapped, not bits within bytes.

Communication between the Macintosh II system and a NuBus card may use any combination of one or more byte lanes. This subject is discussed in more detail under "The Format Block" in Chapter 8; possible byte-lane combinations are shown there in Table 8-2.

Although cards may communicate with each other over the NuBus in any format, all communication with the Macintosh II system (including communication between a card's declaration ROM and the Macintosh II Slot Manager) must conform to the MC68020 bus format. This may require byte swapping when word and long data types are used.

Chapter 5

NuBus Arbitration

This chapter discusses how the bus master is selected from among the several cards likely to be competing for bus mastership, and how all the other cards desiring service are accommodated.

Arbitration overview

The NuBus fair arbitration mechanism differs from strict priority arbitration in that it prevents "starvation" of cards and distributes bus bandwidth evenly.

Arbitrate 3 to arbitrate 0 (/ARB3–/ARB0) are open-collector binary coded lines driven by contenders for the bus. They are used by the distributed arbitration logic to determine bus mastership.

Bus request (/RQST) is an open-collector line driven low by contenders for the bus.

During arbitration, one or more cards contend for control of the NuBus. Cards that desire ownership of the NuBus must first assert the /RQST line. /RQST may be asserted only while it is in an unasserted state. All cards that assert /RQST place their ID codes on the /ARBx lines and contend for the bus. The arbitration logic distributed among the cards determines which of the cards gets ownership of the NuBus. After two clock periods, signal transients have settled and the contest mechanism is complete. The contender with the highest ID code has its code on the /ARBx lines, has won bus ownership, and may initiate a transaction (after completion of any transactions in progress).

Presuming the winner does not desire to lock the bus, the winning card first removes its /RQST and at the same time asserts /START (this begins a start cycle of the card's first transaction). Then, after the start cycle, the card removes its /ARBx signals and continues with the cycles required to complete the transaction.

The release of /START initiates another contest between any cards that originally requested the bus in the same clock period, but that have not yet won. These cards will be granted ownership in turn, from highest ID number to lowest ID number. The rule that /RQST must be unasserted before a card may assert it keeps other cards from participating in contests until all the original requestors have been served.

Figure 5-1 shows a situation in which cards with ID codes $9 and $A request the bus at the same clock period. Card $A wins the first arbitration contest, and then removes its request after its start cycle (when ADR is shown on the /ADx lines). Card $E desires the bus as well but may not request it because the /RQST line is already asserted. Contesting against no one, card $9 wins the next contest and gains bus ownership. When card $9 releases /RQST, card $E requests, arbitrates and wins. Note that card $9 owns the bus only after it both wins a contest and the transaction in progress ends.

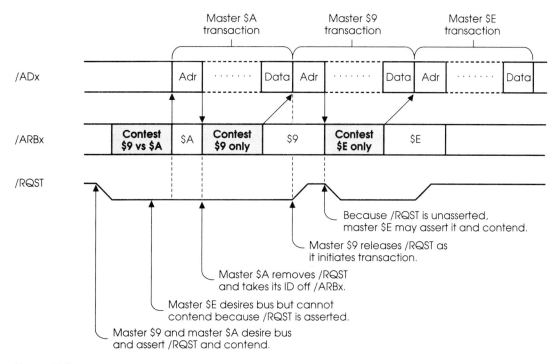

Figure 5-1
Sample arbitration contest

Arbitration logic mechanism

When a bus contest occurs, each card drives the /ARBx lines with its unique ID code and then releases the /ARBx lines if it detects higher ID codes than its own on the /ARBx lines. One possible implementation of this arbitration logic is diagrammed in Figure 5-2, for illustrative purposes only.

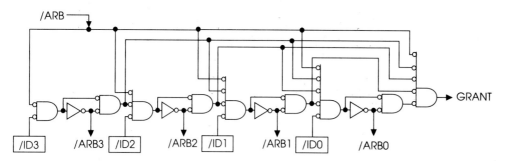

Figure 5-2
Typical bus arbitration logic

Note that the /ARBx lines are bused common to all cards but the /IDx lines present a unique binary code to each card slot. The signals /ARB and GRANT are card signals, not NuBus signals. /ARB is an input to the arbitration logic that indicates whether the card is contending for the bus and GRANT is an output that indicates whether the /ARBx lines currently match this card's /IDx lines. The following logic equations approximate how the arbitration logic on any given card works:

/ARB3 =/ID3 • ARB
/ARB2 =/ID2 • ARB • (/ID3 + ARB3)
/ARB1 =/ID1 • ARB • (/ID3 + ARB3) • (/ID2 + ARB2)
/ARB0 =/1D0 • ARB • (/ID3 + ARB3) • (/ID2 + ARB2) • (/ID1 + ARB1)

where • is Logical AND, + is Logical OR, and ARBx is the logical complement of /ARBx.

According to these equations, after a short delay (arbitration period) the /ARBx lines will equal the ID code of the highest priority contender, that is, the contender with the largest integer for its ID code. See Appendix A for the PAL listing labeled (ARB2), NuBus Arbitration logic; implementation of these equations accomplishes the desired arbitration.

❖ *Note:* The signal names /ARB and GRANT are written here with capital letters, consistent with the convention used in this book, but the Texas Instruments NuBus documentation notates them as "/arb" and "grant," respectively.

General arbitration timing

The details of arbitration timing are covered in Chapter 6, "NuBus Card Electrical Design Guide." Arbitration events generally occur on driving edges and sampling edges, synchronous to the system clock, with the same timing as the basic address/data, control, and utility signals. For example, /RQST may be asserted on a particular driving edge only if it is seen to be unasserted on the previous sample edge. However, the /ARBx lines differ from all other NuBus signals in that their assertion timing is specified from the sample edge of the bus clock. See Figures 5-3 and 6-2.

Single master, bus idle

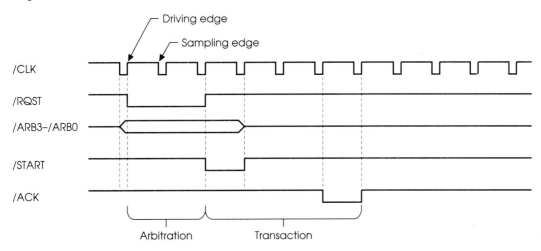

Two masters ($9 & $A), one transaction each

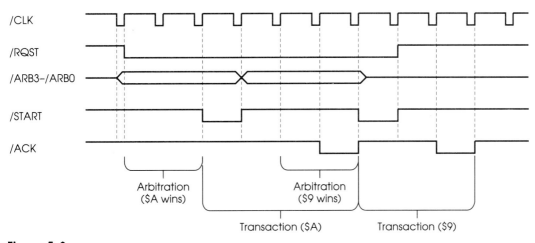

Figure 5-3
NuBus arbitration and transaction timing, single master and two masters

Arbitration contests last two clock periods by definition. On the second sampling edge after a contest starts, all contenders sample their internal grant signal. The highest priority contender will find its GRANT signal asserted. The winner may now take control of the bus and assert /START on the next driving edge (25 ns after the contest's second sampling edge) if the bus isn't in use.

If the bus is in use, the new winner asserts /START on the driving edge immediately after the next sample edge where the current transaction's /ACK is asserted. The new winner continues to assert its ID code on the /ARBx lines throughout the start cycle of its first transaction. This facilitates bus lock detection and bus diagnostics.

Locking

Although cards generally use the bus for a single transaction before allowing another requesting card to become bus master, sometimes the bus must be held locked in an extended tenure. For some local processor operations, it may be necessary to prevent any NuBus requests from interfering with the access of the processsor to its local bus. This might be the case, for example, where the Macintosh II processor is doing an IWM (floppy disk) transfer, which is inherently time critical. Such a processor must have some mechanism (for example, a bus lock line) for locking itself, and its local bus, from NuBus intrusion.

Another example of locking to prevent interference is an indivisible test-and-set operation performed in a multiprocessor environment; this requires a particular condition called a resource lock.

NuBus supports two types of locking: bus locking and resource locking.

Bus locking

Bus locking requires no added mechanism. To lock the bus, a master simply continues to request (by keeping the /ARB lines driven with ID) and contend (continuing to assert /RQST). Because it has the highest ID code of those cards present, it wins subsequent contests. Figure 5-4 shows an example in which card $C locks the bus for two transactions. Fairness in arbitration depends upon cards not locking the NuBus unless required and locking it only for the shortest required tenure.

Any card or software that uses extended-tenure bus locking should clearly specify in the documentation for the product the maximum number of bus cycles allowed.

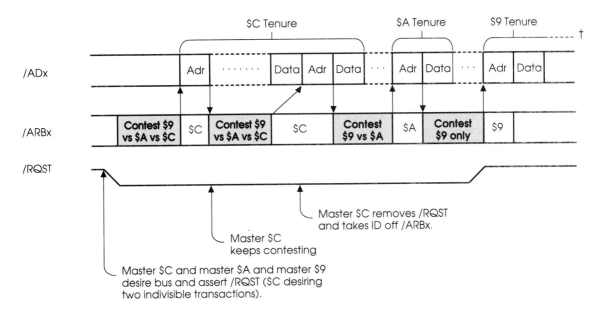

Figure 5-4
Sample bus lock

Resource locking

Resource locking is initiated by the bus owner driving both /START and /ACK to commence an **attention-resource-lock cycle;** this alerts all cards that a bus and resource locked transaction is occurring. The bus lock is maintained as described in the previous section. A bus owner that issues an attention-resource-lock cycle as the first cycle of a bus tenure must conclude that tenure with an attention-null cycle to inform all cards that the tenure is complete.

Access to a resource must be controlled when that resource is accessible by both a local processor and the NuBus. One example of such a shared resource is a dual-ported RAM. Another example is in the Macintosh II, where the NuBus BIU uses the local processor bus to access the shared resource, RAM, as in Figure 5-5.

All cards that have shared resources capable of being locked must monitor the NuBus for an attention-resource-lock cycle and must record the occurrence. A card does not have to react to the occurrence of a bus tenure starting with an attention-resource-lock cycle unless it is addressed during that tenure; this allows multiple resources to be alerted and locked during a single bus tenure.

Figure 5-5 may be helpful in discussing an indivisible bus operation. For example, suppose the processor on the NuBus card is instructed to perform a read-modify-write cycle to the Macintosh II RAM as part of executing a TAS (test and set) instruction. The NuBus card contends for and wins bus ownership, then initiates an attention-resource-lock cycle. The state machines in the BIU respond to the attention-resource-lock cycle by setting a flag. This flag indicates that if the RAM-shared resource is accessed by the processor on the NuBus card, the BIU will lock the the local bus. The Macintosh II local processor will then be unable to access the RAM and thereby interfere with the indivisible read-modify-write of a data structure by the NuBus processor. Any bus owner that is programmed to perform an indivisible bus operation should lock resources on any slaves to be addressed during that operation, as well as locking any bus that provides an alternative path to those resources.

A card is not *required* to provide locking of its local resources; it may do so on some resources and not on others. Reliable TAS instructions may only be done on resources that can be locked.

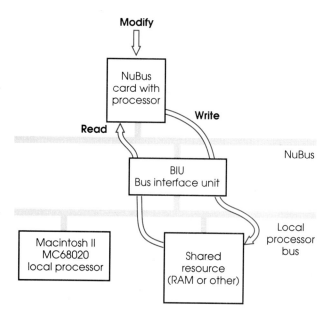

Figure 5-5
Read-modify-write indivisible bus operation

Bus parking

A bus master that has released /RQST is considered **parked** on the bus and may use it at any time (without rearbitration) until another card asserts /RQST. When /RQST is finally asserted by another requestor, the parked bus master finishes its current transaction and relinquishes the bus to the new winner without commencing another transaction. Bus parking reduces the average time to acquire the bus in systems with a small number of contenders.

❖ *Note:* A bus owner is not allowed to go from a parked condition into a bus-locked series of transactions without submitting to arbitration by asserting /RQST.

Chapter 6

NuBus Card
Electrical Design Guide

This chapter provides information on the amount of current your card must supply to drive the NuBus interface and the amount of load you may place on it. A table gives the pin assignments for the 96-pin NuBus expansion connector. Tolerance limits are given for power supply DC and ripple voltages provided to your card. A power budget is provided for allocating current to each slot, at various supply voltages. In conclusion, timing diagrams and tables display the allowable variations in signal transition times.

Electrical requirements

Let's depart from the signal names, logic levels, and memory addresses of earlier chapters and get into volts, ohms, milliamps, and picofarads.

Logical and electrical state relationships

All NuBus signals are active when low. The relationship between logical states and electrical signal levels for all NuBus lines is shown in Table 6-1.

Table 6-1
Logical state definitions

Logical state	Electrical signal level (active low)
H (unasserted)	> 2.0V at the receiver
L (asserted)	< 0.8V at the receiver

DC and AC specifications for line drive

This section provides the drive requirements and the load allowance for each of the NuBus lines. These lines can be divided into five basic types:

- clock
- address/data (/ADx, /SP, /SPV)
- control (/START, /ACK, /TMx)
- open collector (/RESET, /RQST, /ARBx, /NMRQ)
- power control (/PFW)

Table 6-2 lists the specifications for these line (signal) types. Note that the 16 picofarad (pF) AC loading for each of the lines includes the etch and device capacitances only; the capacitive load of the connector need not be included. An additional 2 pF capacitance has been allowed for the connectors mating the Macintosh II logic board to the expansion card. Negative currents indicate flow out of a node (sourcing) and positive currents indicate flow into a node (sinking).

Table 6-2
Bus drivers and receivers

| Signal type | AC drive | | DC drive | | AC load | DC load | |
	I_{PD} (min)	I_{PU} (min)	I_{OL} (min)	I_{OH} (min)	C_L (max)	I_{IL} (max)	I_{IH} (max)
Clock [†]	90mA	50mA	60mA	−30mA	18pF	−1.4mA	0.1mA from driver
Address/data	80mA	40mA	24mA	−12mA @3.2V	18pF	−0.5mA	0.1mA
Control	80mA	40mA	24mA	−12mA @3.2V	18pF	−0.5mA	0.1mA
Open collector	80mA	N/A	60mA	N/A	18pF	−0.625mA	0.1mA
Power control (/PFW) [‡]							

[†] Supplied by the Macintosh II.
[‡] The source of /PFW must be capable of sourcing 20mA at 3V for 2 seconds when driving /PFW high to turn the computing system on. See the next section.

In Table 6-2, the following column headings are used:

I_{PD} Transient pull-down current, required for one T_{pd} whenever the driver changes from unasserted to asserted. See Table 6-6 for T_{pd}.

I_{PU} Transient pull-up current, required for one T_{pd} whenever the driver changes from asserted to unasserted.

I_{OL} Low output drive current available at 0.5V.

I_{OH} High output drive current available at specified voltage.

C_L Capacitive load per slot.

I_{IL} DC low-level input current.

I_{IH} DC high-level input current.

/PFW interaction with the power supply

The /PFW signal is intended to serve two purposes:

1. To allow the power supply to be turned on and off by a low-voltage signal that can be controlled by the logic board (or expansion card) circuitry and hence by software.

2. To allow the power supply to warn the computer of an impending power loss.

When /PFW is held between 3.0 and 6.8 volts for at least 1.5 seconds, the power supply will turn on and the computer will begin operating. Once the power supply turns on, its own +5 volt output holds /PFW high so it can continue operating. If /PFW is pulled below .6 volts, the power supply will turn off; /PFW should be *held* below .6 volts until the computer completely shuts down. If some fault condition (such as AC line failure) causes the power supply to turn off, the power supply will pull /PFW low at least 2 ms before the DC outputs fail.

There are many issues that restrict the circuitry that can be connected to /PFW. Here are a few hints and cautions:

□ The /PFW voltage may be greater than the +5 volt bus voltage for a second or two when the computer is turned on.

□ If /PFW is fed into a gate input, any internal diodes to the +5 volt (or any other power) bus may prevent the computer from turning on because /PFW goes high before the power supply outputs bring the power buses up to rated voltage.

□ No pull up may be added to the /PFW line or else Q4 on the main logic board may not be able to turn off the computer.

□ Any circuitry connected to /PFW must present a high impedance when the power is removed or it may prevent the computer from turning on and drain the battery. Likewise, such circuitry must present a high impedance load during normal operation to prevent contention with other drivers of /PFW. The only time additional circuitry should present a low impedance load to the /PFW line is when it is intentionally and temporarily controlling the /PFW signal.

NuBus connector pin assignments

Table 6-3 gives the pin assignments for NuBus connectors. The order of the rows is given as viewed from the front edge of the card.

Table 6-3
Connector pin assignments

Pin	Row A	Row B	Row C	Pin	Row A	Row B	Row C
1	–12	–12	/RESET	17	/AD23	GND	/AD22
2	‡	GND	‡	18	/AD25	GND	/AD24
3	/SPV	GND	+5	19	/AD27	GND	/AD26
4	/SP	+5	+5	20	/AD29	GND	/AD28
5	/TM1	+5	/TM0	21	/AD31	GND	/AD30
6	/AD1	+5	/AD0	22	GND	GND	GND
7	/AD3	+5	/AD2	23	GND	GND	/PFW
8	/AD5	†	/AD4	24	/ARB1	†	/ARB0
9	/AD7	†	/AD6	25	/ARB3	†	/ARB2
10	/AD9	†	/AD8	26	/ID1	†	/ID0
11	/AD11	†	/AD10	27	/ID3	†	/ID2
12	/AD13	GND	/AD12	28	/ACK	+5	/START
13	/AD15	GND	/AD14	29	+5	+5	+5
14	/AD17	GND	/AD16	30	/RQST	GND	+5
15	/AD19	GND	/AD18	31	/NMRQ	GND	GND
16	/AD21	GND	/AD20	32	+12	+12	/CLK

† These pins are connected but not supplied with the –5.2V described in the Texas
  Instruments NuBus specification. This voltage could be supplied by a card, in which case
  –5.2V would be available to all cards.

‡ These pins are RESERVED in the standard IEEE 1196; in the Macintosh II, they are
  grounded.

Power supply specifications

Three voltages are specified on the NuBus: +5, +12, and –12 volts. These voltages are listed in Table 6-4 with their specifications.

Table 6-4
Power supply specifications

Source label	Nominal value	Tolerance from nominal	Combined line and load regulation	Maximum ripple (peak-peak)
+5	5V	±3%	0.3%	50mV
+12	12V	±3%	0.3%	75mV
–12	–12V	±3%	0.3%	75mV

NuBus power budget

The maximum current available to any one NuBus card is one sixth of that available to the entire NuBus. Worst case analysis for a fully loaded Macintosh II, with equal current allocation to each of the six slots, yields the recommendations in Table 6-5. A similar analysis, starting with the maximum capacitance for which the power supply operates reliably and subtracting the maximum capacitance on the main logic board, yields the card filter capacitance recommendations in the table.

Table 6-5
Recommended current and capacitance limits for a NuBus card

Nominal power supply value	Recommended maximum current per card (slot)	Recommended maximum capacitance per card
5V	2.0A, continuous	1513 microFarads
12V	0.175A, continuous	536 microFarads
–12V	0.150A, continuous	698 microFarads

❖ *Note:* The current analysis assumed a hard disk (1.8A RMS max.) and two floppy disk drives (0.2A typical) internal to the Macintosh II; if you choose to develop a card which exceeds these recommendations, you should make the end user aware of any limitations imposed on the system configuration.

The recommendations for maximum card capacitance are actual (not nominal) capacitance. You must allow for the capacitance tolerances of the particular capacitors being used in order to stay below the recommended maximum.

Timing requirements

To meet the following timing requirements, you must pay careful attention to card construction practices. It is important that you provide adequate design and manufacturing margins so that cards manufactured by you and other developers may be interchangeably inserted in any Macintosh II computer and all communicate with each other and the MC68020 processor on the main logic board.

Utility and data transfer timing

Figure 6-1 shows the clock, control, and address/data timing relationships during data transfers. Table 6-6 lists the bus timing specifications for these signals. The abbreviations used in Figure 6-1 are defined in Table 6-6.

Control and address/data signals are changed on the rising edge of /CLK and sampled on the falling edge of /CLK. This timing gives protection from bus skew.

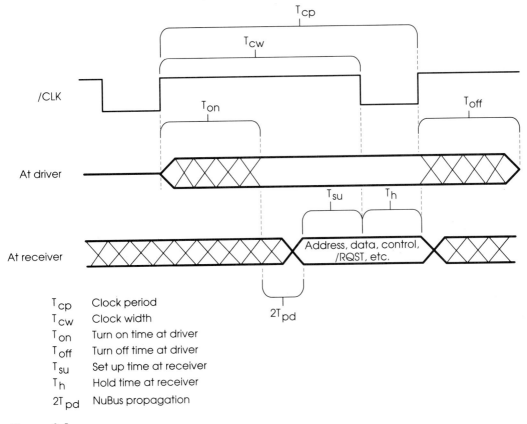

T_{cp}	Clock period
T_{cw}	Clock width
T_{on}	Turn on time at driver
T_{off}	Turn off time at driver
T_{su}	Set up time at receiver
T_h	Hold time at receiver
$2T_{pd}$	NuBus propagation

Figure 6-1
Data transfer timing

Table 6-6
Bus timing summary

Parameter	Description	Minimum	Maximum	Units
T_{cp}	Clock period	99.99	100.01	ns
T_{cw}	Clock width	73	77	ns
T_{on}	Turn-on time	0	35	ns
T_{off}	Turn-off time	0	35	ns
$2T_{pd}$	NuBus delay	—	17	ns
T_{su}	Setup time	21	—	ns
T_h	Hold time	$T_{cp}-T_{cw}$	—	ns

Setup, hold, and other times are defined at the card-to-NuBus connectors. All card-internal delays must be taken into account while providing for the times specified in the table.

Arbitration timing

Refer to Chapter 5, "NuBus Arbitration," for a description of the arbitration process. The timing for the /ARBx signals is not the same as the timing of the data transfer signals. Arbitration begins on the falling (sampling) edge of /CLK before the assertion of /RQST or, if /RQST is already active on the falling edge of /CLK, during /START. The contenders assert their respective slot ID's on the /ARBx lines. The bus contest must be settled within two cycles of /CLK following the assertion of /RQST or the negation of /START. By the end of that interval, the /ARB lines will contain the ID code of the card winning the arbitration contest.

Figure 6-2 details the /ARBx timing for an arbitration won by card $A (1010) following a /START signal initiated by card $9 (1001). See Table 6-7 for the meaning of the abbreviations used in Figure 6-2.

In the general case, contenders must wait for the preceding bus master to release the /ARBx line before the succeeding bus arbitration can take place. Thus, the arbitration turn-on time (T_{on}) for /ARBx signals is the turn-off time of the preceding master (T_{off}), plus the bus propagation delay ($2T_{pd}$, one reflection assumed), plus the time taken to react to the change in logic levels (T_{en}).

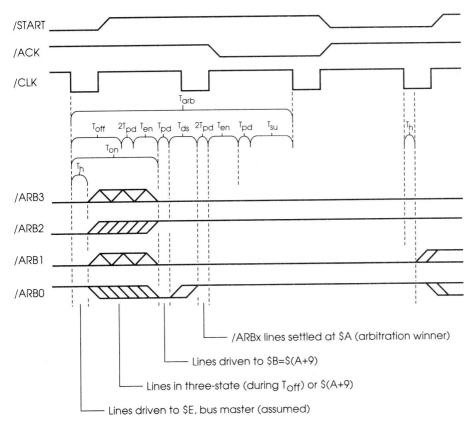

Figure 6-2
Detailed arbitration timing

Table 6-7 lists the timing specifications for the /ARBx lines.

Table 6-7
Bus arbitration timing summary

Parameter	Description	Minimum	Maximum	Units
T_{arb}	Arbitration time	—	200	ns
T_{on}	Arbitration turn-on time	10	83	ns
T_{ds}	Arbitration disable time	—	26	ns
T_{en}	Arbitration enable time	—	26	ns
T_{su}	Arbitration setup time	31	—	ns
T_h	Hold time	10	—	ns
T_{off}	Turn-off time	10	40	ns
$2T_{pd}$	NuBus delay	—	17	ns

EMI guidelines for expansion cards

The Macintosh II computer meets FCC radio and television electromagnetic interference (EMI) requirements as a stand-alone device, or when connected to a peripheral device such as a printer or modem. However, you should follow certain guidelines to avoid exceeding the mandatory FCC limits when the Macintosh II is expanded as follows:

☐ an expansion card is mounted internally using the NuBus connector, with no external I/O connections

☐ an expansion card is mounted internally using the NuBus connector *and* external I/O connections are provided

Without external I/O connections

The following guidelines should enable you to build an add-on that does not degrade the Macintosh II to the extent that the combination product will not meet FCC regulations for Class B equipment. However, you are responsible for the FCC authorization of the combination product. Development testing should be undertaken as soon as a realistic expansion card is available, in order to alert you, the developer, to any serious EMI problems. These problems can be resolved by re-routing signal conductors, filtering and bypassing, and eliminating excessive transient ringing (undershoot) on clocks and other signals by providing the proper terminations for buses. Appropriate emission control techniques must be used on the card and on wiring to any connectors for external I/O.

☐ Use cards with four layers (power and ground on two layers), or with extremely low impedance busing of power and ground lines, so that the EMI pick-up and emanations will be reduced.

☐ Buffer high speed signals and separate them from lower speed circuitry.

☐ Buffer signals from the 96-pin connector as close to the connector as possible and limit the drive to one LS load with a maximum of 30 pF capacitance.

☐ Internal interconnecting cables should be as short as possible. Position cables such that inductive and capacitive coupling with the Macintosh II subassemblies is minimized. You should not bundle conductors carrying high-speed signals with conductors carrying low-speed signals. In certain cases, you may have to use internal shielding or twisted pairs within cables.

☐ Do not locate high-speed components such as clock oscillators and their signal lines near the expansion port connector and shield.

☐ Cards require good high frequency decoupling in addition to adequate power supply filtering at their low-voltage power connectors. These precautions avoid degrading the low emission levels conducted from the Macintosh II 120V power connector.

With external I/O connections

Connecting a cable to an external I/O connector can seriously compromise the emissions integrity built into the Macintosh II. You are likely to exceed allowable limits on conducted or radiated emissions unless you take care during construction and test of *the total system as it will be operated.* The total system includes

□ the unmodified Macintosh II

□ the expansion card and all internal cables used to modify the Macintosh II

□ the external cable and peripherals to be connected

It is very important for you to consider the following:

□ Follow all the guidelines given for internal expansion cards as described previously.

□ Include EMI filtering in each I/O and power line going to or beyond (outside) the I/O connector. This is best achieved by using deglitch packs (RC or LC networks) or common mode chokes located directly at the connector.

□ Shape the spectrum of signals, especially video, in the frequency domain so that unrequired bandwidth and harmonics are not needlessly propagated. (Note: Computer designers tend to prefer very fast edges so that timing errors are never a problem, but it is these very fast edges that cause high amplitude harmonics in the frequency domain and lead to emission problems.)

□ Use a good quality connector, one that has high conductivity (electrical) plating and accepts a shielded plug. The tin-plated steel DB series of connectors is one obvious example. The connector should be mechanically and electrically bonded to the metal I/O fence on the rear of the expansion card. An unsecured, unbonded connector protruding through the plastic aperture is almost sure to cause a major EMI problem.

□ External metal conductor cables must be shielded, without exception. Solder bond the entire circumference of the braided shield to provide a low impedance path to the entire perimeter of the connector.

□ Interconnecting cables should be as short as possible. Do not bundle conductors carrying high-speed signals with conductors carrying low speed signals. In certain cases, you may have to use internal shielding or twisted pairs within cables.

Chapter 7

NuBus Card
Physical Design Guide

This chapter contains physical design guidelines for the development of Macintosh II expansion cards. It describes the personal computer style card for insertion into a NuBus connector and gives the dimensional ranges allowed. (A much larger, triple-height style is also specified in Texas Instruments documentation.) Heat dissipation and product safety guidelines conclude the chapter.

Card description

Foldout 1 at the back of the book is a drawing showing the pertinent details of a NuBus card, particularly the overall dimensions and the placement of connectors.

Warning

Foldout 1 is from a design guide used within Apple Computer and was correct at the time of publication. Future updates may be made available through APDA, the Apple Programmer's and Developer's Association.

Cards must be 4.0 inches in height and between 12.875 and 7.0 inches in length. Foldout 1 shows a Macintosh II card, viewed from the component side. The NuBus connector is on the bottom edge of the card in the drawing. The I/O connector is on the right side.

Card thickness must be 0.062 ± 0.0075 inches. Warpage must be controlled to within 0.10 inch deviation from ideal.

Components may be placed anywhere within the unslashed area of Foldout 1. The prohibited area along the top edge in the figure applies to cards of any length.

Components may not extend beyond the edge of the card, in any direction. Component height must not extend more than 0.60 inch, measured from the card surface. No component or wire lead is allowed to extend more than 0.10 inch beyond the non-component side of the card.

Cards must be spaced at least 0.900 inch apart. The nominal spacing between centerlines of adjacent NuBus connectors in the Macintosh II is 0.900 inches.

You can purchase blank Macintosh II expansion cards for prototyping from

Diversified I/O, Inc.
1008 Stewart Drive
Sunnyvale, CA 94086
(408) 730-2171
AppleLink Address: D0242

NuBus connector description

The NuBus connector on the card must be a 603-2-IEC-C096-M connector. Pin assignments are as shown earlier in Table 6-3. Figure 7-1 shows the version of that connector used on the Macintosh II Video Card. The mating connector on the Macintosh II main logic board is the same as the connector used in the Macintosh SE and shown in Figure 14-6.

A source of Euro-DIN connectors meeting Apple specifications is

AMP Incorporated
Harrisburg, PA 17105

Because of high volume production requirements, Apple purchases specially modified versions of the Euro-DIN connector from this vendor. However, you may purchase mating connectors of standard configuration from this or other vendors.

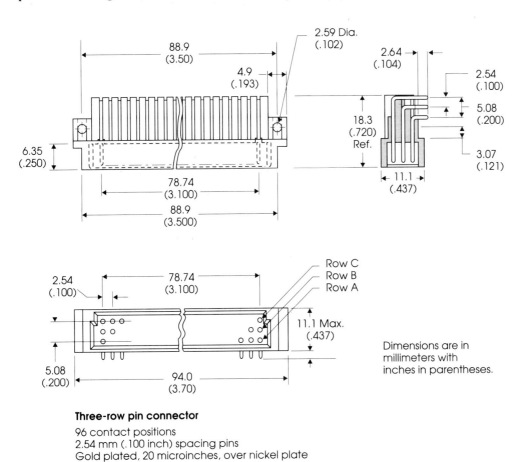

Three-row pin connector

96 contact positions
2.54 mm (.100 inch) spacing pins
Gold plated, 20 microinches, over nickel plate

Dimensions are in millimeters with inches in parentheses.

Figure 7-1
96-pin plug connector for a Macintosh II expansion card

A metal shield surrounds the I/O connector on the rear of the card, for EMI protection. Chapter 6, "NuBus Card Electrical Design Guide," contains guidelines for EMI reduction when the Macintosh II is expanded. See Foldout 2 at the back of the book for a drawing of the I/O connector shield.

Warning

Foldout 2 is from a design guide used within Apple Computer and was correct at the time of publication. Future updates may be made available through APDA, the Apple Programmer's and Developer's Association.

The type and number of I/O connectors (if required) is left to you, but they must meet dimensional constraints of the shield.

An auxiliary connector is allowable, but discouraged. It must be located as shown in Foldout 1 and be no longer than 3.0 inches.

Heat dissipation guidelines

Macintosh II expansion cards, by their own heat dissipation, will produce increased temperatures within the Macintosh II. Because excessive heat can have a detrimental effect on performance and reliability, Apple recommends the following guidelines:

1. Dissipation by the expansion card of up to 13.3 watts of power provides a comfortable margin for the major Macintosh II components. This total is arrived at as follows:

+5V @ 2.0A =	10.0W	
+12V @ 0.175A =	2.1W	
−12V @ 0.1A =	1.2W	
Total power =	13.3W	

   Dissipation of more than 13.3 watts of power by a card may cause excessive temperature rise on certain critical components. Apple studies indicate that at an ambient temperature of about 24°C, 13.3 watts of dissipated power from the expansion card will cause an acceptable rise in average component case temperature to about 53°C. (Studies were conducted with an internal hard disk drive installed.)

2. You can achieve optimum cooling for both the logic board and expansion cards by keeping the expansion card as short as possible; the minimum possible is 7.0 inches (see the section titled "Card Description," earlier in this chapter). In addition, placing larger components near the bottom side of the expansion card is desirable.

3. Place hot components on the expansion card directly against the board; they should have the widest possible printed wiring traces. This provides for better cooling by the air flow from the fan, moving from the rear of the Macintosh II to the front.

4. Installation of an expansion card should not cause the case temperature of an internal hard disk to rise more than 20°C over external ambient air temperature.

5. Internally mounted disk products should not cause the air temperature inside the Macintosh II case to rise more than 20°C over external ambient air temperature.

Product safety

The Macintosh II computer meets national and international product safety requirements. Therefore, any additional cards and components need careful safety consideration to maintain the same degree of electrical and mechanical safety. When you, as a third party developer, manufacture an expansion card that is designed to fit inside the Macintosh II, you must consider several product safety issues.

The Macintosh II is approved by American (Underwriters Laboratories—UL), Canadian (Canadian Standards Association—CSA), and European (Institute for Industrial Research and Standards—IIRS) regulatory organizations in a configuration with dummy expansion cards. When you change the design of the product by adding a functional expansion card, and resell the unit, essentially the product becomes delisted. Technically, you should resubmit the Macintosh II with your card installed and have the new (combination) product evaluated. The new product should have a new model number and the Macintosh II essentially becomes a component of your system.

You can maintain product safety if you follow these guidelines:

□ Stay within the maximum power specification of the expansion connector.

□ Use components that have been certified by the safety agencies. Components such as lithium batteries, power relays, tape drives, disk drives, fans, wires and cables, and other parts should have at least UL and CSA approvals.

□ Properly secure (mount) the components. Avoid mountings that depend on adhesive only or mountings that allow movement of components or cards.

□ Avoid using materials that could contribute to a fire. This includes PCB material, card guides, and other parts. In general, PCB material should be flame rated 94V-1 or better, wire should be UL Listed/CSA Certified, flame rated VW-1, and plastic parts within the enclosure should be flame rated 94V-2 or better.

□ Place PCBs and other components so that they do not block vent openings or fan circulation.

- Secure all wiring and provide chafing protection to prevent degradation of the insulation on moving parts or sharp edges.

- Do not configure connectors such that a hazard is created if they are plugged in backwards or into the wrong connector.

- Avoid splicing of wires. Conversion kits should provide new harnesses if they are required.

- Avoid soldering. If soldering is necessary, the connection should be made mechanically secure before soldering (no tack soldering).

- Installation or conversion instructions must be complete. Provide a review by a person who is unfamiliar with the product to insure that instructions are complete and accurate enough for that person to understand.

The following guidelines apply particularly to expansion cards that use *high voltages.*

- Do not allow maintenance work to be performed by persons not knowledgeable of the hazards involved.

- Be careful to maintain proper through-air and over-surface spacings between the high voltage components (power supply, relays, and so forth) and the logic circuitry. Remember that spacings are measured under worst case conditions and that if a card can be moved, spacings will be measured with the card in the worst position. Spacing tables can be found in the the following safety standards: UL478, CSA 22.2 No. 154-M1983, CSA 22.2 No. 220-M1986, IEC 380, IEC 435, and IEC 950.

- Maintain proper insulation thickness or layers between the high voltage components and the logic circuitry. (Proper insulation is defined in the standards listed in the preceding item.) If a low voltage circuit can contact a high voltage wire, the low voltage wire must also be insulated for the higher voltage.

- Avoid placement of components next to high voltage parts.

Chapter 8

NuBus Card Firmware

This chapter describes the firmware that must be included on cards that communicate with the Macintosh II through the NuBus protocol. Such firmware is normally in a ROM area on the card called the **declaration ROM.** A card's declaration ROM area can be implemented in any of three different physical widths: 8, 16, or 32 bits.

The system routines that communicate with the card's declaration ROM are contained in the Macintosh II ROM, in a section called the **Slot Manager.** For details about the Slot Manager, see *Inside Macintosh,* Volume V.

The discussion in this chapter is divided into the following parts:

☐ a list of the data types used by the Slot Manager and the card firmware

☐ a description of the required internal structure of the card firmware

☐ a section of examples

Data types

Table 8-1 shows the data types used for communication between the Slot Manager and the card firmware. Two of the data types are illustrated in Figure 8-1.

Table 8-1
Data types

Data type	Description
Byte	8 bits, signed or unsigned
Word	16 bits, signed or unsigned
Long	32 bits, signed or unsigned
Pointer	32 bits, signed or unsigned
cString	One-dimensional array of bytes, the last of which has the value $00
Offset	24 signed bits padded to 32 bits, representing a self-relative offset; only bytes in valid byte lanes are counted
sBlock	See Figure 8-1
SExecBlock	See Figure 8-1

sBlock

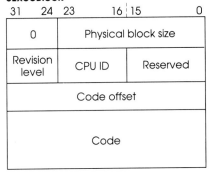

0	Physical block size
	Data structure

SExecBlock

31	24	23	16	15	0

0	Physical block size
Revision level	CPU ID	Reserved
Code offset	
Code	

Figure 8-1
Formats of sBlock and SExecBlock data types

❖ *Note:* Whenever offset values are used in the declaration ROM firmware, they count only bytes in byte lanes actually being used. Hence these values may be less than the arithmetic difference between the two addresses being offset. For a discussion of byte lanes, see "NuBus Bit and Byte Structure" in Chapter 4.

Firmware structure

The firmware contained in a card's declaration ROM defines one or more slot resources (**sResources**) unique to that card. Each sResource is associated with a specific capability of the card.

Don't confuse sResources on plug-in cards with standard Macintosh resources; they are different, although related conceptually. Every sResource has a type and a name. If it is device-oriented, it may also have an icon and driver code in firmware, and may define a region of system memory allocated to the card it is in. Some sResources, however, may contain only data—for example, special fonts.

When a NuBus card controls multiple hardware devices, it usually contains separate sResources for each device in its declaration ROM. Special fields in the sResource list, defined below, let you identify the specific hardware and software associated with each sResource.

In addition to the sResources themselves, every NuBus card's declaration ROM firmware must include these elements:

□ a **format block**

□ an **sResource directory**

□ a **Board sResource list**

□ one or more other **sResource lists,** one for each sResource on the card

The relation among these elements is diagrammed in Figure 8-2.

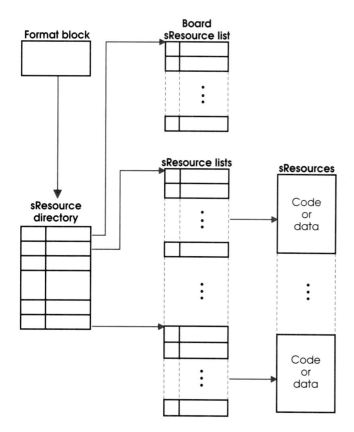

Figure 8-2
Card firmware

Additional diagrams of simple and complex NuBus card firmware structures are given under "Examples," at the end of this chapter.

The format block

The format block starts at the highest address of the declaration ROM and follows at immediately lower addresses, counting only those addresses accessed by valid byte lanes. Byte lanes are discussed in the next section. The overall format block structure is shown in Figure 8-3.

	Number of bytes
ByteLanes	1
Reserved	1
TestPattern	4
Format	1
RevisionLevel	1
CRC	4
Length	4
DirectoryOffset	4

Figure 8-3
Format block structure

The first byte of the format block must reside at one of the four bytes at the end of the slot space defined under "Slot Allocations" in Chapter 4—that is, the format block must begin with a NuBus address in the range $FsFF FFFF through $FsFF FFFC, where s is the slot number. The actual starting address used depends on the value of the ByteLanes field, as discussed in the next section.

When the Macintosh II is started up, the Slot Manager searches its six slots for installed cards, as described in the Device Manager chapter of *Inside Macintosh,* Volume V. For each slot it first searches NuBus addresses $FsFF FFFF–$FsFF FFFC (where s is the slot number), looking for a valid ByteLanes value. It then verifies this value by examining the TestPattern field. If no valid ByteLanes and TestPattern values are found, the Slot Manager stores a slot error in the corresponding sInfo record, as described under "The Slot Manager" in *Inside Macintosh,* Volume V.

The format block also contains format and identification information and ends with an offset to the sResource directory. The individual fields of the format block are discussed in the sections that follow.

ByteLanes

The ByteLanes field tells the Macintosh II which of the four NuBus byte lanes to use when communicating with the card's declaration ROM. NuBus byte lanes are defined under "NuBus Bit and Byte Structure" in Chapter 4. The value of ByteLanes is composed by setting a bit in the low nibble for each byte lane used and then setting the high nibble to the low nibble's complement. The location of the first bit set to 1 in the low nibble also determines the address of ByteLanes, and hence the starting address of the format block. Table 8-2 shows all the possible ByteLane values and their corresponding format block starting addresses (where s is the slot number). Notice that the ByteLanes byte always occupies the highest address available in the byte lanes being used. The Slot Manager will refuse to recognize any ByteLanes values not shown in Table 8-2.

Table 8-2
Possible ByteLanes values

Byte lanes used	ByteLanes value	Address of ByteLanes
0	$E1	$FsFF FFFC
1	$D2	$FsFF FFFD
0,1	$C3	$FsFF FFFD
2	$B4	$FsFF FFFE
0,2	$A5	$FsFF FFFE
1,2	$96	$FsFF FFFE
0,1,2	$87	$FsFF FFFE
3	$78	$FsFF FFFF
0,3	$69	$FsFF FFFF
1,3	$5A	$FsFF FFFF
0,1,3	$4B	$FsFF FFFF
2,3	$3C	$FsFF FFFF
0,2,3	$2D	$FsFF FFFF
1,2,3	$1E	$FsFF FFFF
0,1,2,3	$0F	$FsFF FFFF

Reserved

The Reserved field must be set to $00.

TestPattern

The TestPattern field identifies the format block. It must be set to $5A93 2BC7.

Format

The one-byte Format field identifies the declaration ROM format. A format value of $01 designates the Apple format defined in the file DeclROMEqu.a.

RevisionLevel

This one-byte RevisionLevel field identifies the current ROM revision. The Slot Manager accepts RevisionLevel values in the range 1–9. RevisionLevel values above 9 cause it to generate a fatal error in the form of a status value of –303.

CRC

The four-byte Cyclic Redundancy Check value constitutes a checksum to allow the Slot Manager to validate the whole declaration ROM. It is computed by applying a 32-bit rotate-left-and-add function to the number of bytes specified by the Length field. Only the bytes specified by the ByteLanes field are used to calculate the CRC value. For example, if the value of ByteLanes is $E1 the calculation would use only the bytes at addresses $FsFF FFFC, $FsFF FFF8, $FsFF FFF4, and so on. In making the CRC computation, the value of CRC itself is treated as 0. Here is the basic algorithm:

```
Start pointer at bottom of ROM (top of ROM – length)
Initialize sum to 0 (sum will be the calculated CRC value)
@ 1      Rotate sum left by one bit (with ROL.L #1 instruction)
         If pointer is pointing to the CRC field in the format header, goto @2
         Get the byte pointed to by pointer
         Add the byte to sum
@ 2      Increment pointer to next data byte
Goto @1 until done (as specified by length bytes)
```

Length

The Length field contains a long value specifying the number of bytes from the declaration ROM's starting address (as specified by the ByteLanes value) to the lowest-address byte of the sResource data structures.

DirectoryOffset

The long DirectoryOffset value specifies the self-relative signed offset from the offset itself to the sResource directory. It counts only the bytes in the NuBus byte lanes being used, not the absolute address difference.

Examples

Figure 8-4 shows two examples of the actual structure of a format block, with the actual addresses that would be used if the card were installed in slot 9. The structure on the left assumes that only byte lane 1 is used; the structure on the right assumes byte lanes 0, 2, and 3 are used.

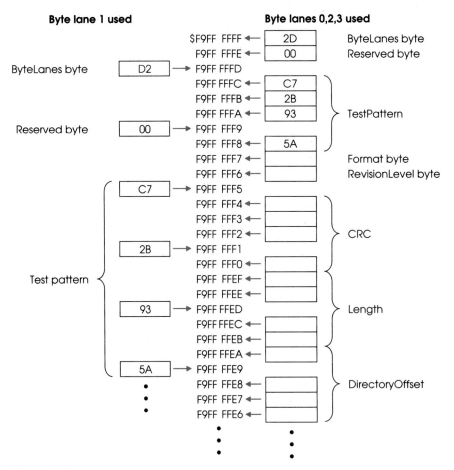

Figure 8-4
Format block examples

The sResource directory

The sResource directory lists all the sResource lists in the card firmware and provides an offset (counting only valid byte lane bytes) to each one.

Each sResource list defined by a card designer must have an identification number in the range 128–254 that is not duplicated within that card's declaration ROM. Identification number 255 is used as an end-of-list marker.

Identification numbers in the sResource directory and in every sResource list must be in ascending order.

❖ *Note:* Identification numbers in the range 0 to 127 are reserved for sResource lists required by the Slot Manager. At present there is only one of these: the Board sResource list described later in this chapter.

The sResource directory structure is shown in Figure 8-5.

ID

sRsrcId-0	Offset
sRsrcId-1	Offset
⋮	⋮
sRsrcId-n	Offset
End of list	0

Figure 8-5
sResource directory structure

Each entry in the sResource directory (except the end-of-list entry) points to an sResource list. Each entry consists of 32 bits, allocated as follows:

31–24   sResource identification number
23–0   Offset from the entry to the sResource list, counting only valid byte lanes

The last entry in the sResource directory must have an offset of 0 and an identification number of 255; that is, it must have the value $FF00 0000.

sResource lists

Each sResource list contains a set of references to information about a single sResource. This information must include the type and name of the resource; it may also include the resource's icon, driver, and parameters. Its driver is also required if the sResource is a startup resource or may be a startup video source.

The general form of an sResource list is shown in Figure 8-6.

ID

sRsrc_Type	Offset
sRsrc_Name	Offset
sRsrcIcon	Offset or data
⋮	⋮
End of list	0

Figure 8-6
sResource list structure

Each entry in an sResource list must have one of the following three forms:

Offset	Bits 31–24	Identification number
	Bits 23–0	Offset to Long data, cString, sBlock, or another list
Word	Bits 31–24	Identification number
	Bits 23–16	$00
	Bits 15–0	Word data
Byte	Bits 31–24	Identification number
	Bits 23–8	$00 00
	Bits 7–0	Byte data

The data types mentioned above are defined under "Data Types" at the beginning of this chapter.

The last entry in every sResource list must have the value $FF00 0000.

Identification numbers for sResource list entries defined by the card designer must be in the range 128–254. They identify items accessed by driver or application code. Identification numbers in the range 0–127 are reserved by Apple; those currently assigned to certain standard Apple sResource list entries are shown in Table 8-3. Notice that every sResource list must have entries with ID numbers 1 and 2; the other entries are all optional. Entries must be listed in ascending numerical order.

Table 8-3
Apple sResource list ID numbers

Name	ID number	Description
sRsrc_Type	1	Type of the sResource (required)
sRsrc_Name	2	Name of the sResource (required)
sRsrc_Icon	3	Icon for the sResource
sRsrc_DrvrDir	4	Driver directory for the sResource
sRsrc_LoadRec	5	Load record for the sResource
sRsrc_BootRec	6	Boot record
sRsrc_Flags	7	sResource flags
sRsrc_HWDevId	8	Hardware device ID
MinorBaseOS	10	Offset to the base of the sResource in slot space
MinorLength	11	Length of the sResource in slot space
MajorBaseOS	12	Offset to the base of the sResource in super slot space
MajorLength	13	Length of the sResource in super slot space

The sResource list entries listed above are described in the next section. Slot and super slot addressing spaces are discussed under "Address Space" in Chapter 4.

Standard sResource list entries

This section describes the standard Apple sResource list entries recognized by the Slot Manager. The sRsrc_Type and sRsrc_Name entries are required; the others are optional.

sRsrc_Type

The type entry in an sResource list is used by the Macintosh II Operating System or by an application or driver to identify the type of the sResource. It is required. The actual value of the entry in the sResource list is an offset to an eight-byte format defined by Apple. This format is designed to cover all possible devices that might be supported by a card in a Macintosh II slot. However, a bit flag in the format allows the card designer to substitute any other format. The sResource type format is shown in Figure 8-7.

Warning
Non-Apple sResource type formats may conflict with each other. If possible, you should use only the Apple format and Apple-assigned values.

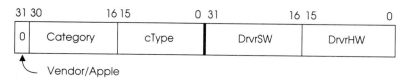

Figure 8-7
sResource type format

The fields in the Apple sResource type format are as follows:

Vendor/Apple   The vendor/Apple flag bit must be cleared to 0 for Apple format.

Category   The Category is the most general classification of card functions. Categories include display, network, terminal emulator, serial, parallel, intelligent bus, and human input devices.

cType   The cType is a subclass within a category. Within display devices, for example, are video cards and graphics extension processors; within networks, AppleTalk® and Ethernet.

DrvrSW   The DrvrSW field identifies the driver software interface for the sResource. It also specifies how parameters are stored in the sResource list.

DrvrHW   The DrvrHW field identifies the hardware associated with the sResource and its driver interface.

The value of each sResource type is unique and is assigned by Apple. To obtain sResource type values for the card you are designing, contact Apple Technical Support.

sRsrc_Name

The sRsrc_Name entry in an sResource list provides the name of the sResource. It is required. The actual value of the entry in the sResource list is an offset to a cString not more than 254 characters long. The routine sGetDrvrName, described later in this chapter, prefixes a period to the value of the cString and converts its type to Str255. The name should be the sResource type string; for example, 'catDisplay_TypVideo_DrSWApple_DrHWTFB'.

sRsrc_Icon

The sRsrc_Icon entry in an sResource list provides the icon for the sResource. The actual value of the entry in the sResource list is an offset to a resource of type 'ICON'.

sRsrc_DrvrDir

An sRsrc_DrvrDir or sRsrc_LoadRec entry is required in an sResource list if the sResource needs a driver to be installed in the Macintosh II Operating System before 'INIT' 31 resources are called. Otherwise both are optional. An sRsrc_DrvrDir entry is required if the driver for the sResource resides in the card's declaration ROM; a sRsrc_LoadRec is required if it resides in an external location, such as a hard disk attached to the card.

The actual value of the sRsrc_DrvrDir entry in the sResource list is an offset to an sDriver directory. Each entry in the sDriver directory contains an offset to an sDriver record, an sBlock containing the driver code. The identification number for each entry specifies which operating system supports the driver. Table 8-4 gives the standard sDriver directory identification numbers.

Table 8-4
sDriver directory ID numbers

Name	ID number	Description
sMacOS68000	1	Driver will run on a Macintosh family with MC68000 processor
sMacOS68020	2	Driver will run on a Macintosh family with MC68020 processor

Other identification numbers may be used for future Macintosh family operating systems.

Figure 8-8 shows a typical sDriver directory.

ID

sDRVRId-1	Offset
sDRVRId-2	Offset
⋮	⋮
sDRVRId-n	Offset
End of list	0

Figure 8-8
Typical sDriver directory

sRsrc_LoadRec

Either an sRsrc_LoadRec entry or an sRsrc_DrvrDir entry (but not both) is required in an sResource list if the sResource needs a driver to be installed in the Macintosh II Operating System before 'INIT' 31 resources are called; otherwise both are optional. The sRsrc_DrvrDir entry is discussed in the preceding section.

The actual value of the sRsrc_LoadRec entry in the sResource list is an offset to an sLoadDriver record. The sLoadDriver record has the format of an SExecBlock and contains the code necessary to load the appropriate driver. The SExecBlock is described under "Data Types" at the beginning of this chapter.

sRsrc_BootRec

The sRsrc_BootRec entry in an sResource list is an offset to an sBootRecord. The sBootRecord is needed whenever the Macintosh II starts from a NuBus card instead of from the internal hard disk or floppy drive. Either the Macintosh Operating System or an entirely different operating system can be installed from a card using the sBootRecord.

The sBootRecord has the same format as an SExecBlock. The structure of the SExecBlock is described under "Data Types" at the beginning of this chapter.

The Macintosh II will attempt to start from a NuBus card only when certain values are set in its parameter RAM. These values can be accessed by using the Start Manager, as described in *Inside Macintosh,* Volume V.

If an sResource with the specified ID in the specified slot exists, and that sResource has an sBootRecord, it is used for startup. Otherwise, the normal Macintosh startup process occurs.

The sBootRecord code is first called early in the ROM-based startup sequence, before any access to the internal drive. It is passed an seBlock pointed to by register A0. If a non-Macintosh operating system is being installed, the sBootRecord can pass control to it. In this case, control never returns to the normal start sequence in the Macintosh ROM.

When the Macintosh Operating System is started up, the sBootRecord is called twice. The first time, when the value of seBootState is 0, the startup code tries to load and open at least one driver for the card-based device and install it in the disk drive queue. It returns the refnum of the driver or an error status. That driver becomes the initial one used to install the Macintosh Operating System. During the second call to the sBootRecord, which happens after system patches have been installed but before 'INIT' resources have been executed, the sBootRec must open any remaining drivers for devices on the card.

The sBootRecord can use the HOpen call to open the driver and install it into the unit table. The HOpen call will either fetch the driver from the sDriver directory, or call the sLoadDriver record if one exists. In any case, the driver's open code must install the driver into the drive queue.

The sBootRecord uses the following SExecBlock fields:

seBootState = 0

→	seSlot	The slot number (from parameter RAM)
→	seRsrcID	The sResource ID (from parameter RAM)
→	seDevice	The device number (from parameter RAM)
→	sePartition	The partition number (from parameter RAM)
→	seOSType	Type of operating system to boot (from parameter RAM)
→	seReserved	A reserved field (from parameter RAM)
→	seBootState	0
←	seRefNum	Returned refnum of driver to boot with
←	seStatus	Returned status (zero = good, negative = no driver loaded)

seBootState = 1

→	seSlot	The slot number
→	seRsrcID	The sResource ID
→	seDevice	0
→	sePartition	0
→	seOSType	Type of operating system (from parameter RAM)
→	seReserved	A reserved field (from parameter RAM)
→	seBootState	1

sRsrcFlags

The only flag at present in the sRsrcFlags word entry is fOpenAtStart. True tells the Start Manager to install and open the driver at startup time; false tells it to leave the driver closed. If there is no sRsrcFlags entry, fOpenAtStart is assumed true by default. All unused flags must be set to 0.

sRsrcHWDevId

The sRsrcHWDevId byte entry identifies the sResource as a hardware device. If the sResource is not a hardware device (for example, a data structure), this entry may be omitted. Each hardware device must be given a unique ID.

MinorBaseOS

The MinorBaseOS entry in an sResource list contains an offset to a long value that defines the sResource's entry point in the slot space allocated to the slot its card is in. The long value is an offset relative to NuBus address $Fs00 0000, where s is the slot number. Slot space and super slot space are discussed under "Address Space" in Chapter 4.

MinorLength

The MinorLength entry in an sResource list contains an offset to a long value representing the number of bytes of slot space addressed by the sResource.

MajorBaseOS

The MajorBaseOS entry in an sResource list contains an offset to a long value that defines the sResource's entry point in the super slot space allocated to the slot its card is in. The long value is an offset relative to NuBus address $s000 0000, where s is the slot number.

MajorLength

The MajorLength entry in an sResource list contains an offset to a long value representing the number of bytes of super slot space addressed by the sResource.

The Board sResource list

This section describes the **Board sResource list,** a standard Apple sResource list that must be present in the firmware for every card that communicates with the Macintosh II. The Board sResource list provides the Macintosh II with a card's identification number, vendor information, board flags, and initialization code. For an illustration of how the Board sResource list is used, see the section "Examples" at the end of this chapter.

Table 8-5 gives the standard identification numbers assigned to the Apple-defined entries in the Board sResource list.

Table 8-5
Apple-defined entry ID numbers

Name	ID number	Description
BoardId	32	Card design identification number
PRAMInitData	33	Data for initializating the PRAM bytes for the slot
PrimaryInit	34	Primary initialization code
STimeOut	35	TimeOut constant
VendorInfo	36	Vendor part number, name, and so forth

These entries are described in the following sections. Within the same Board sResource list you must add entries for sRsc_Type and sRsc_Name, which are required in every sResource list. You can also add others of the resource references described earlier, such as sRsc_Icon.

BoardId

The BoardId entry in the Board sResource list is required; without it, the Macintosh II will log an error in the appropriate sInfo record. The boardId value is a word (two bytes) assigned by Apple. To obtain one for the card you are designing, contact Apple Technical Support.

PRAMInitData

There are six bytes reserved in the Macintosh II PRAM for each slot. The PRAMInitData entry lets you specify values other than zero for these bytes. If it is present in the Board sResource list it provides an offset to an sBlock called an sPRAMInit record, which contains PRAM initialization values. If it is omitted from the Board sResource list, the PRAM bytes will be initialized to zero. Initialization occurs when the Macintosh II Operating System detects a card for the first time or when the Slot Manager finds a BoardId in a Board sResource that is different from the BoardId in the corresponding sPRAMInit record.

The structure of the sPRAMInit record is shown in Figure 8-9.

31 24	23 0		
0	Physical block size		
0	0	Byte 1	Byte 2
Byte 3	Byte 4	Byte 5	Byte 6

Figure 8-9
sPRAMInit record structure

PrimaryInit

The PrimaryInit entry in a Board sResource list contains an offset to a PrimaryInit record. The PrimaryInit record has the format of an SExecBlock containing the code neccessary to initialize the card. The structure of the SExecBlock is given under "Data Types" at the beginning of this chapter.

If the PrimaryInit record is not present, the Macintosh II assumes that the card initializes itself or does not require initialization.

A pointer to an seBlock is passed in register A0 to the PrimaryInit code. This parameter block indicates the slot and sResource ID to the PrimaryInit code.

You must observe the following restrictions when writing code for the PrimaryInit record:

☐ The code may make no calls to the Macintosh firmware except the Slot Manager.

☐ The code's length must be less than 2048 bytes.

☐ The code's execution time must be less than 200 milliseconds.

Initialization code that exceeds these requirements can be placed in the Open routine of a driver provided for the card.

The code is expected to return a status in the seStatus field of the SExecBlock data structure. This value is saved in the siInitStatusV field of the sInfo record for the slot. Zero or positive values indicate no error or non-fatal errors. Negative values indicate a fatal error occured while initializing the card; they prevent the Slot Manager from accessing the card and set an error value in the siInitStatusA field of the sInfo record.

TimeOut

The TimeOut constant is an option for cards capable of locking out the 68020 processor. If the Slot Manager detects a lockout condition, it will retry the number of times specified by TimeOut. If TimeOut is not specified, a default value of 100 will be used.

VendorInfo

The optional VendorInfo entry in a Board sResource list contains an offset to a VendorInfo list. The Macintosh II does not use the data in this structure. Vendor information should be placed in cStrings and use the standard identification numbers shown in Table 8-6.

Table 8-6
VendorInfo list ID numbers

Name	ID number	Description
VendorID	1	The card vendor's design identification
SerialNum	2	The individual card's serial number
RevLevel	3	The card design's revision level
PartNum	4	The part number of the card
Date	5	Last revision date of the card

Example

Figure 8-10 diagrams a typical Board sResource list.

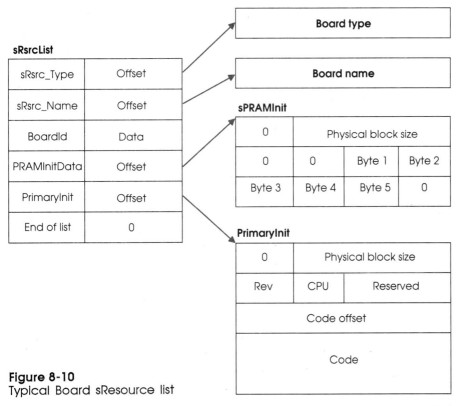

Figure 8-10
Typical Board sResource list

Sample code

Here is a sample of firmware code for a typical NuBus card, using the Macintosh Programmer's Workshop assembly language.

```
;-------------------------------------------------------------------------------
;
;   General structure:
;
;                              [Format/Header]
;                                    |
;                                    |
;                            [sResource Directory]
;                             /                \
;                            /                  \
;                           /                    \
;                          /                      \
;              [Board sResource]          [Video sResource]
;               - Primary Init             - Driver Directory
;               - Vendor Info              - Parameters for 1, 2 & 4-bit modes
;
;-------------------------------------------------------------------------------


;===============================================================================
;                        Initial Assembler Directives
;===============================================================================
            STRING      C
            PRINT       OFF
            LOAD        'inc.sum.d'
            INCLUDE     'nSysEqu.a'         ;Get JVBLTask
            INCLUDE     'DeclROMEqu.a'      ;Declaration ROM EQU's
            INCLUDE     'SlotMgrEqu.a'      ;Slot Manager EQU's
            INCLUDE     'SlotMgrMacs.a'     ;Slot Manager macros
            INCLUDE     'SlotIntEqu.a'      ;Slot interrupt equates
            INCLUDE     'IndVideoEQU.a'     ;Independent video equates
            INCLUDE     'DepVideoEQU.a'     ;Dependent video equates
            INCLUDE     'colorequ.a'        ;color equate file.
            PRINT       ON


;===============================================================================
;                              Macros
;===============================================================================

; Offset List Entry
            MACRO
            OSLstEntry  &Id,&Offset
            DC.L        (&Id<<24)+&Offset-*
            ENDM

; Data List Entry
            MACRO
            DatLstEntry &Id,&Data
            DC.L        (&Id<<24)+&Data
            ENDM
```

```
;================================================================================
;       BEGIN Declaration ROM
;================================================================================
VideoDeclROM    MAIN

;================================================================================
;                       Directory
;================================================================================
_sRsrcDir       OSLstEntry      sRsrc_Board,_sRsrc_Board        ;References the Board sResource
                OSLstEntry      sRsrc_Video,_sRsrc_Video        ;References the video sResource
                DatLstEntry     EndOfList,0                     ;End of the list

;================================================================================
;                       sRsrc_Board List
;================================================================================
_sRsrc_Board    OSLstEntry      sRsrc_Type,_BoardType           ;References the sResource type
                OSLstEntry      sRsrc_Name,_BoardName           ;References the sResource name
                DatLstEntry     BoardId,TFBBoardId              ;The board Id
                OSLstEntry      PrimaryInit,_sPInitRec          ;References the Primary init
                                                                ;record
                OSLstEntry      VendorInfo,_VendorInfo          ;References the Vendor information
                                                                ;list
                DatLstEntry     EndOfList,0                     ;End of the list.

_BoardType      DC.W            CatBoard                        ;The Board sResource :<Category>
                DC.W            TypBoard                        ;                     <Type>
                DC.W            0                               ;                     <DrvrSw>
                DC.W            0                               ;                     <DrvrHw>
_BoardName      DC.L            'Sample video card'             ;The name of the board should
                                                                ; be the official product name

;--------------------------------------------------------------------------------
;                       Primary Init Record
;--------------------------------------------------------------------------------
_sPInitRec      DC.L            _EndsPInitRec-_sPInitRec        ;The physical Block Size
                INCLUDE         'PrimaryInit.a'                 ;The Header/Code (See
                                                                ;PrimaryInit.a)
_EndsPInitRec   EQU             *                               ;End of block
                STRING          C                               ;Restore to 'c' string type

;--------------------------------------------------------------------------------
;                       Vendor Info record
;--------------------------------------------------------------------------------
_VendorInfo     OSLstEntry      VendorId,_VendorId              ;References the Vendor Id
                OSLstEntry      RevLevel,_RevLevel              ;References the Revision Level
                OSLstEntry      PartNum,_PartNum                ;References the Part Number
                DatLstEntry     EndOfList,0                     ;End of the list

_VendorId       DC.L            'XYZ Inc.'                      ;The Vendor Id
_RevLevel       DC.L            'Beta-7.0'                      ;The Revision Level
_PartNum        DC.L            'TFB-1'                         ;The Part Number
```

```
;==========================================================================================
;                              sRsrc_Video
;==========================================================================================
_sRsrc_Video    OSLstEntry      sRsrc_Type,_VideoType           ;References the sResource Type
                OSLstEntry      sRsrc_Name,_VideoName           ;References the sResource Name
                OSLstEntry      sRsrc_DrvrDir,_VidDrvrDir       ;References the driver directory
                DatLstEntry     sRsrc_HWDevId,1                 ;The hardware device ID

                OSLstEntry      MinorBaseOS,_MinorBase          ;References the Minor Base Offset
                OSLstEntry      MinorLength,_MinorLength         ;References the Minor Base Length

;Parameters
                OSLstEntry      OneBitMode,_OneBitMode          ;References 1-bit mode parameters
                OSLstEntry      TwoBitMode,_TwoBitMode          ;References 2-bit mode parameters
                OSLstEntry      FourBitMode,_FourBitMode        ;References 4-bit mode parameters

                DatLstEntry     EndOfList,0                     ;End of the list.

_VideoType      DC.W            CatDisplay                      ;Video sResource :    <Category>
                DC.W            TypVideo                        ;                     <Type>
                DC.W            DrSwApple                       ;                     <DrvrSw>
                DC.W            DrHwTFB                         ;                     <DrvrHw>

_VideoName      DC.L            'Display_Video_Apple_TFB'       ;Convention: _VideoName is derived
                                                                ;by using _VideoType above, but
                                                                ;stripping off the Cat,Typ, and
                                                                ;DrSw/Hw prefixes, then
                                                                ;separating by underscores

_MinorBase      DC.L            defMinorBase                    ;Video RAM Offset is 0
_MinorLength    DC.L            defMinorLength                  ;Video RAM length is $40000

;------------------------------------------------------------------------------------------
;                       Driver directory
;------------------------------------------------------------------------------------------
_VidDrvrDir     OSLstEntry      sMacOS68020,_sMacOS68020        ;References the Macintosh-OS 68020
                                                                ;driver
                DatLstEntry     EndOfList,0                     ;End of the list

;Driver-1 (68020)
_sMacOS68020    DC.L            _End020Drvr-_sMacOS68020        ;The physical Block Size
                INCLUDE         'TFBDrvr.a'                     ;The Header/Code (See TFBDrvr.a)
_End020Drvr     EQU             *                               ;The end of the driver
                STRING          C

;------------------------------------------------------------------------------------------
;                       One-bit-per-pixel parameter list.
;------------------------------------------------------------------------------------------
_OneBitMode     OSLstEntry      mVidParams,_OneVidParams        ;References the one-bit mode
                                                                ;parameter record
                DatLstEntry     mPageCnt,4                      ;The page count
                DatLstEntry     mDevType,defmDevType            ;The device type
                DatLstEntry     EndOfList,0                     ;End of the list
```

```
_OneVidParams  DC.L            _EndOneVParams-_OneVidParams ;The physical Block Size.

               DC.L            defmBaseOffset
               DC.W            1024/8                       ;Bounds.R*PixelSize/8
               DC.W            defmBounds_T,defmBounds_L,defmBounds_B,defmBounds_R
               DC.W            defVersion                   ;bmVersion
               DC.W            0                            ;packType not used
               DC.L            0                            ;packSize not used
               DC.L            defmHRes                     ;bmHRes
               DC.L            defmVRes                     ;bmVRes
               DC.W            defPixelType                 ;bmPixelType
               DC.W            1                            ;bmPixelSize
               DC.W            defCmpCount                  ;bmCmpCount
               DC.W            1                            ;bmCmpSize
               DC.L            defmPlaneBytes               ;bmPlaneBytes

_EndOneVParams EQU             *                            ;End of block.

;-------------------------------------------------------------------------------
;                     Two-bits-per-pixel parameter list.
;-------------------------------------------------------------------------------
_TwoBitMode    OSLstEntry      mVidParams,_TwoVidParams     ;References the two-bit mode
                                                            ;parameter record.
               DatLstEntry     mPageCnt,2                   ;The page count.
               DatLstEntry     mDevType,defmDevType         ;The device count.
               DatLstEntry     EndOfList,0                  ;End of the list.

_TwoVidParams  DC.L            _EndTwoVParams-_TwoVidParams ;Physical Block Size.

               DC.L            defmBaseOffset
               DC.W            1024*2/8                     ;Bounds.R*PixelSize/8
               DC.W            defmBounds_T,defmBounds_L,defmBounds_B,defmBounds_R
               DC.W            defVersion                   ;bmVersion
               DC.W            0                            ;packType not used
               DC.L            0                            ;packSize not used
               DC.L            defmHRes                     ;bmHRes
               DC.L            defmVRes                     ;bmVRes
               DC.W            defPixelType                 ;bmPixelType
               DC.W            2                            ;bmPixelSize
               DC.W            defCmpCount                  ;bmCmpCount
               DC.W            2                            ;bmCmpSize
               DC.L            defmPlaneBytes               ;bmPlaneBytes

_EndTwoVParams EQU             *                            ;End of block.

;-------------------------------------------------------------------------------
;                     Four-bits-per-pixel parameter list.
;-------------------------------------------------------------------------------
_FourBitMode   OSLstEntry      mVidParams,_FourVidParams    ;References the four-bit mode
                                                            ;parameter record.
               DatLstEntry     mPageCnt,1                   ;The page count.
               DatLstEntry     mDevType,defmDevType         ;The device type.
               DatLstEntry     EndOfList,0                  ;End of the list.
```

```
_FourVidParams DC.L           _EndFourVParams-_FourVidParams     ;Physical Block Size.

               DC.L           defmBaseOffset
               DC.W           1024*4/8                           ;Bounds.R*PixelSize/8
               DC.W           defmBounds_T,defmBounds_L,defmBounds_B,defmBounds_R
               DC.W           defVersion                         ;bmVersion
               DC.W           0                                  ;packType not used
               DC.L           0                                  ;packSize not used
               DC.L           defmHRes                           ;bmHRes
               DC.L           defmVRes                           ;bmVRes
               DC.W           defPixelType                       ;bmPixelType
               DC.W           4                                  ;bmPixelSize
               DC.W           defCmpCount                        ;bmCmpCount
               DC.W           4                                  ;bmCmpSize
               DC.L           defmPlaneBytes                     ;bmPlaneBytes

_EndFourVParams EQU           *                                  ;End of block.

               ORG            ROMSize-fhBlock.fhBlockSize
;============================================================================================
;                   Format/Header Block
;============================================================================================
               DC.L           (_sRsrcDir-*)**$00FFFFFF           ;Offset to sResource directory
               DC.L           ROMSize                            ;Length of declaration data
               DC.L           0                                  ;CRC {Patched by crcPatch, an MPW
                                                                 ;tool}
               DC.B           Rev1                               ;Revision level
               DC.B           AppleFormat                        ;Format
               DC.L           TestPattern                        ;Test pattern
               DC.B           0                                  ;Reserved byte (must be zero)
               DC.B           $E1                                ;ByteLanes: 1110 0001 (bytelane 0)

               ENDP

               END
```

Chapter 9

NuBus Card Driver Design

In most cases, using a card that communicates with the Macintosh II computer through the NuBus protocol requires a driver routine in the system software. General guidelines for writing drivers are given in the Device Manager chapters of *Inside Macintosh,* Volumes II, IV, and V. This chapter supplements that information with some specific notes about NuBus card drivers and gives you an example.

You have three choices for storing the driver code for a NuBus card:

☐ It may be stored as an sDriver record in the card firmware. In this case, the driver code is loaded onto the Macintosh II system heap immediately before 'INIT' resources are executed, unless specifically inhibited by the fOpenAtStart bit in the sRsrc_Flags field being set to 0. The sDriver record is described later in this chapter.

☐ It can be fetched by an sLoadDriver record, in which case the driver code may be stored virtually anywhere. The sLoadDriver record is discussed under "sRsrc_LoadRec" in Chapter 8.

☐ It may be stored in an 'INIT' 31 resource in the System Folder on a disk that accompanies the NuBus card. In this case, it is installed during system startup as described in the Device Manager chapters of *Inside Macintosh,* Volumes II, IV, and V.

Regardless of where it is stored, a NuBus card driver may be written either for a specific card or for a class of cards. These two approaches are discussed in the first part of this chapter.

Finally, there are certain special requirements that video card drivers must meet, in addition to the general driver requirements outlined in *Inside Macintosh.* These are discussed in the last part of this chapter.

This chapter ends with a pseudocode example of a NuBus video card driver interface and a quick-reference summary of the code and data structures described in the text.

Specific and generic drivers

A NuBus card driver may be written in either of two ways:

☐ It may be hard-coded to refer to a specific card.

☐ It may be written to refer generically to cards of a certain class.

These two approaches are discussed in this section.

Card-specific drivers

A **card-specific driver** contains in its code all the critical information required for it to drive a specific card. For example, if the driver were associated with a video card it might contain bits-per-pixel information and control register addresses. It could then be used to drive only cards of a specific configuration, as specified by the sRsrc_Type field of the sResource.

The way such a driver would work with the card hardware and firmware is diagrammed in Figure 9-1.

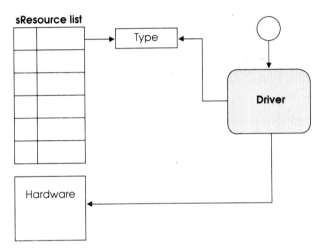

Figure 9-1
Card-specific driver

Card-generic drivers

A **card-generic driver** interrogates the appropriate sResource list in the card firmware to determine the hardware configuration with which it must work. The sResource list is discussed in Chapter 8. For example, a driver associated with a class of video cards might obtain bits-per-pixel information and control register addresses from an sResource in the card's declaration ROM, using Slot Manager calls. The Slot Manager is described in *Inside Macintosh,* Volume V.

The way such a driver would work with the card hardware and firmware is diagrammed in Figure 9-2.

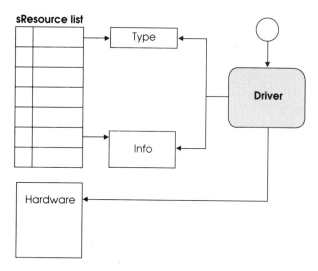

Figure 9-2
Card-generic driver

❖ *Note:* You can easily design a video-card declaration ROM that designates multiple video devices—for example, devices that work with different sizes of video RAM. At startup time, all devices are inserted into the slot device table. Then during initialization (before any screen display), the system can determine the size of the available RAM on the video card and delete all but one device.

The sDriver record

When a driver is stored in the firmware of its associated card, it is placed in an sDriver record. An sDriver record is a record of type sBlock, as defined under "Data Types" in Chapter 8. Its general form is shown in Figure 9-3. The specific structure of the driver header and driver routine sections depends on the operating system with which the driver works. For the Macintosh family Operating Systems, this structure is described under "The Structure of a Device Driver" in the Device Manager chapter of *Inside Macintosh*, Volume II.

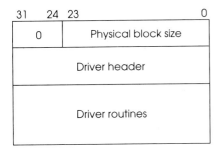

Figure 9-3
sDriver record

Installing a driver at startup

During its startup process, the Macintosh II Operating System searches the NuBus slots looking for device drivers to install. As described in Chapter 8, the declaration ROM area of each card contains an sResource directory that points to all the sResource lists in that card's firmware. For each sResource list that refers to a device, the corresponding sResource may contain either actual device driver code or code that allows a driver to be loaded from an external source.

❖ *Note:* The system file may contain drivers for current Apple-designed NuBus cards. Card vendors who supply drivers should use the 'INIT' 31 resource to install them during startup. The 'INIT' 31 resource is described in the System Resource File chapter of *Inside Macintosh*, Volume IV.

For each sResource, the search for drivers during startup takes place in the following steps:

1. The Operating System looks for an sRsrc_Flags field in the sResource list.

2. If no sRsrc_Flags field exists, or if an sRsrc_Flags field exists and the field's fOpenAtStart bit is set to 1, the Operating System searches for a driver, as described below in steps 3–4. If the value of fOpenAtStart is 0, the Operating System does not search for a driver; it goes on to the next sResource.

3. The system searches the sResource list for a driver load record (sRsrc_LoadRec)—a routine designed to copy a driver into the Macintosh system heap. If such a routine exists, the system copies it from the card's ROM to the heap and executes it. The system passes this routine a pointer in A0 to an seBlock; on exit, the routine must return a handle in the seResult field of the same seBlock to the driver it has loaded. If the value of the seStatus field is 0, the system then installs the new driver.

4. If there is no driver load record, the system searches the sResource list for a driver directory entry (sRsrc_DrvrDir). If there is such an entry and the directory contains a driver of the type sMacOS68000 or sMacOS68020, the system reads the driver from the card's ROM and installs it in the Macintosh system heap.

This method lets you design a card with its driver in ROM on the card. The user can then plug the card in the machine and use the device without running an installation program. Should the driver in ROM later require updating, you can supply an 'INIT' file to be added to the user's system folder. The 'INIT' file can test the existing driver version and override it with a version contained in its own code, thereby substituting a new driver for the old one.

❖ *Note:* For this method to work correctly, you must follow all the rules for slot card drivers. In particular, you must include the version number (word-aligned) immediately after the driver's name.

The video driver used at the beginning of system startup (the one that makes the "happy Macintosh" appear) must be taken from a video card's declaration ROM because the system file is not yet accessible. If a system contains multiple video cards, the one used first is determined by parameter RAM or, by default, by selecting the lowest slot number. To override this initial driver, the user must install an 'INIT' 31 resource that explicitly closes the driver from the declaration ROM and loads a new driver from a file.

❖ *Note:* As a consequence of the foregoing, any video card that contains the only video device in a system, or supplies the startup device, must have at least a minimal video driver in its configuration ROM.

To install a driver, the Macintosh II ROM first loads it into the system heap and locks it if the dNeedsLock bit in the driver flags (drvrFlags) word is set. It then installs the driver with a DrvrInstall system call and initializes it with an Open call. If the driver returns an error from the Open call, it is marked closed, the refNum field is cleared in the ioParameter block, and the driver is unlocked. Note that this procedure guarantees that driver initialization code will be executed before the system starts executing applications.

Calling a driver

In the Macintosh II, the low-level PBOpen routine has been extended to let you open devices in NuBus slots. If the slot serves a single device (not, for example, a chain of disk drives), set the value of ioFlags to 0 and use the following parameter block:

→	12	ioCompletion	Pointer
←	16	ioResult	Word
→	18	ioNamePtr	Pointer
←	24	ioRefNum	Word
→	27	ioPermssn	Byte
→	28	ioMix	Pointer
→	32	ioFlags	Word
→	34	ioSlot	Byte
→	35	ioId	Byte

In the extension fields, ioMix is a longint reserved for use by the driver open routine. The ioSlot parameter contains the slot number of the device being opened, in the range $9–$E; if a built-in device is being opened, ioSlot must be 0. The ioId parameter contains the sResource ID.

If the slot serves more than one device, set the value of ioFlags to fMulti and use the following parameter block:

→	12	ioCompletion	Pointer
←	16	ioResult	Word
→	18	ioNamePtr	Pointer
←	24	ioRefNum	Word
→	27	ioPermssn	Byte
→	28	ioMix	Pointer
→	32	ioFlags	Word
→	34	ioSEBlkPtr	Pointer

Here the new parameter ioSEBlkPtr is a pointer to an external parameter seBlock that is customized for the devices installed in the slot. The pointer value is passed to the driver. The seBlock structure is described in the Slot Manager chapter of *Inside Macintosh,* Volume V.

When a driver serves a device that is plugged into a NuBus slot, it needs to know the slot number, the sResource ID number, and the ExtDevID number within the slot. The Slot Manager provides values for several new entries on the end of the Device Control Entry (DCE) data structure for each sResource. These new entries are

□ a byte containing the slot number (dCtlSlot)

□ a byte containing the sResource ID number for the sResource (dCtlSlotID)

□ a pointer to the device base address (dCtlDevBase) for the driver to use

□ a reserved pointer field for future use (dCtlReserved)

□ a byte containing the external device ID (dCtlExtDev)

Use of the base address pointer dCtlDevBase in the DCE is required if it refers to a video sResource; otherwise it is optional. On a card with multiple instances of the same device, the driver can use this pointer to distinguish among devices. Because the DCE address is passed to the driver on every call from the Device Manager, the presence of this pointer in the DCE simplifies location of the correct device. This pointer is loaded with a relocated version of the sRsrcMinBase field from the device's sResource list before the driver is called. This frees the driver writer from the necessity of locating the hardware for simple slot devices. The system makes no other references to this field.

Slot device interrupts

Slot interrupts come in on the Macintosh II VIA2 chip, which contains an 8-bit register that has a bit for each slot. This means that there is effectively one interrupt line per card. You can tell almost instantly which card requested the interrupt, but not which device on the card. To locate the interrupt to a device, the Slot Manager provides a slot polling procedure.

The Device Manager maintains an interrupt queue for each slot. Upon receipt of a slot interrupt, the Device Manager goes through the slot's interrupt queue until it gets an indication that the interrupt has been satisfied. If no such indication occurs, an error dialog, similar to that for system errors, is displayed.

The format for a slot queue element is the following:

```
SQLink      EQU     0       ;Link to next element (pointer)
SQType      EQU     4       ;queue type ID for validity (word)
SQPrio      EQU     6       ;priority (low byte of word)
SQAddr      EQU     8       ;interrupt service routine (pointer)
SQParm      EQU     12      ;optional A1 parameter (long)
SQSize      EQU     16      ;length of slot queue element
```

The SQPrio field is an unsigned byte that determines the order in which slots are polled and routines are called. Higher value routines are called sooner. Priority values 200–255 are reserved for Apple devices.

The SQParm field is a value that is loaded into register A1 before calling an interrupt service routine. This is normally the address of the driver's DCE.

The 256K Macintosh II ROM's Device Manager provides two new routines to implement the interrupt queue process just described: SIntInstall and SIntRemove.

sIntInstall

```
FUNCTION SIntInstall(sIntQElemPtr: SQElemPtr; theSlot: INTEGER ): OsErr;
```

Trap macro   _SIntInstall

SIntInstall adds a new element (pointed to by sIntQElemPtr) to the interrupt queue for the slot whose number is given in theSlot. As explained in the Slot Manager chapter of *Inside Macintosh,* Volume V, slots are numbered from $9 to $E. SIntInstall returns an error if it is unsuccessful.

From assembly language, this routine has the following calling sequence:

```
        LEA         MySQE1,A0               ;Get slot queue element
        LEA         PollRoutine,A1          ;Get routine address
        MOVE.L      A1,SQAddr(A0)           ;Set address
        MOVE.W      Prio,SQPrio(A0)         ;Set priority
        MOVE.L      A1Parm, SQParm(A0)      ;Save A1 parameter
        MOVE.W      Slot,D0                 ;Set slot number
        _SIntInstall                        ;Do installation
```

This code causes the routine at label PollRoutine to be called as a result of an interrupt from the specified slot ($9–$E). The Device Manager polls the slot that has the highest priority first if two or more slots request an interrupt simultaneously.

sIntRemove

```
FUNCTION SIntRemove(sIntQElemPtr: SQElemPtr; theSlot: INTEGER): OsErr;
```

Trap macro   _SIntRemove

SIntRemove removes an element (pointed to by sIntQElemPtr) from the interrupt queue for the slot whose number is given in theSlot. SIntRemove returns an error if it is unsuccessful.

From assembly language, this routine has the following calling sequence:

```
        LEA         MySQE1,A0               ;Pointer to queue element
        _SIntRemove                         ;Remove it
```

This routine lets you remove an installed driver containing an interrupt handler from the system without causing a crash.

PollRoutine

Your driver polling routine is called with the following assembly-language code:

```
MOVE.L        SQParm(A0),A1            ;Load A1 Parameter
JSR           (A1)                     ;Call polling routine
```

Your polling routine should preserve the contents of all registers except A1 and D0. It should return to the Device Manager with an RTS instruction. D0 should be set to zero to indicate that the polling routine did not service the interrupt, or nonzero to indicate the interrupt has been serviced. The polling routine should not set the processor priority below 2, and should return with the processor priority equal to 2. The Device Manager resets the VIA2 int flag and and executes an RTE to the interrrupted task when a polling routine indicates that the interrupt is satisfied.

Video drivers

If a NuBus card controls a video display device, there are additional requirements its driver must satisfy. The system recognizes that a NuBus card has a video capability by examining the sRsrc_Type fields of its sResource lists.

To be recognized by the Macintosh II system, every video sResource must have an associated driver in the Macintosh II system heap. This driver may either be loaded from the card's ROM by the Slot Manager, or supplied separately on disk.

Besides using its driver, there are two other ways the Macintosh II system communicates with a video card:

□ Its driver must provide a pointer to the card's video RAM, which QuickDraw then accesses directly. Writing pixel information directly into RAM is faster than using driver calls.

□ The Slot Manager retrieves information directly from a card's declaration ROM. Such information may include definitions of its potential display modes, as well as data of any kind placed there by the card designer. The declaration ROM data required in video cards is defined in the next section.

Video card firmware normally contains an initialization routine, as described in Chapter 8. The initialization routine should set the video card to a startup mode of one bit per pixel, using page 0. It should also clear the video RAM to either the color gray or a 50% gray stipple pattern. The driver's Open routine may then set the video card to any configuration desired. After the default video driver is opened, it is set to the mode defined by byte 2 in the sPRAM record for the card. The user can change this byte by means of the Control Panel.

Video declaration ROM information

The data structures required in the declaration ROM of any NuBus card are described in Chapter 8. Among them is the sResource list, which contains the sResource type, name, and other information about a device. For each mode a video sResource supports, the sResource list should contain a reference to a mode list. Such references must begin at ID 128 and continue in ascending order. ID 128 identifies the default mode if a mode is not specified in the sPRAM record. The parameter IDs for mode list entries are shown in Table 9-1.

Table 9-1
Video driver parameter IDs

Name	ID number	Description
mVidParams	1	Video device record ID
mTable	2	Offset to the table
mPageCnt	3	Number of pages for video display in 1-bit mode
mDevType	4	Device type

The declaration ROM for a video card defines any alternate operating modes for that card. Each mode is completely identified by the following four parameters:

☐ the number of the slot in which it is installed

☐ the sResource identification number of the video device it drives

☐ the identification number of the mode

☐ the contents of vidData

Each distinct mode must have its own video device record, with the structure shown in Table 9-2. This structure is the same as the PixMap structure described in the Color QuickDraw chapter of *Inside Macintosh,* Volume V, except that it describes the physical configuration of a device, not a pixel image.

Table 9-2
Video device record

Name	Size	Description
vpBaseOffset	Long	Offset to page 0 of video RAM (from MinorBaseOS)
vpRowBytes	Word	Width of each row of video memory
vpBounds	4 words	BoundsRect for the video display (gives dimensions)
vpVersion	Word	PixelMap version number
vpPackType	Word	Unused
vpPackSize	Word	Unused
vpHRes	Long	Horizontal resolution of the display device (pixels per inch)
vpVRes	Long	Vertical resolution of the display device (pixels per inch)
vpPixelType	Word	Defines pixel type: chunky = 0, planar = 1 (see Color QuickDraw chapter in *Inside Macintosh,* Volume V)
vpPixelSize	Word	Number of bits in pixel
vpCmpCount	Word	Number of components in pixel
vpCmpSize	Word	Number of bits per component
vpPlaneBytes	Long	Offset from one plane to the next

For general information about video card sResource entries, see the section "Standard sResource List Entries" in the Slot Manager chapter of *Inside Macintosh,* Volume V.

❖ *Note:* A video card feature you may wish to include is one that disables its declaration ROM if no monitor is plugged into the card. You can do this by enabling the video ROM through a sensing circuit in the monitor's connector.

Video driver routines

General instructions for writing device drivers are given in the Device Manager chapters of *Inside Macintosh,* Volumes II, IV, and V. This section discusses only requirements specific to video drivers.

Normally, a driver associated with a Macintosh II card may reside either in the card's declaration ROM or on disk. But video drivers differ from other drivers in that they should be able to support screen displays soon after the system is started up, before any code is read from disk. Hence for video cards it is desirable that at least a rudimentary driver reside in the declaration ROM. Such a driver would be loaded during initialization and display at least one bit per pixel. This would let the Macintosh II display messages during the startup process.

At a minimum, any video driver must support Open, Close, Control, and Status calls from the Macintosh II Operating System. Your driver's Open routine must accomplish the following:

□ allocate any private data storage required by the driver

□ store a handle to its private data space in the dCtlStorage field of the driver's device control entry

□ initialize any local variables that the driver uses

□ install an interrupt handler for the driver

□ enable VBL interrupts on the video card

❖ *Note:* The Operating System does not expect that your driver's Open routine will set or change the video mode. The Start Manager explicitly sets the appropriate video mode during startup as determined by parameter RAM or by an 'scrn' resource (described in the Color QuickDraw chapter of *Inside Macintosh,* Volume V).

Your video driver's Close routine must accomplish the following:

□ disable VBL interrupts on the video card

□ remove the interrupt handler used by the driver, replacing any changed interrupt vectors

□ release any private data storage held by the driver

Any data to be preserved until the next time the video driver is opened should be stored in the relocatable block of memory pointed to by dCtlStorage.

Video driver data structures

The Macintosh II Operating System communicates with each video driver by means of control and status calls that use the following data structures:

```
TYPE

VDEntRecPtr = ^VDEntryRecord;
VDEntryRecord = RECORD
                    csTable: Ptr;           {pointer to color lookup table}
                    csStart: INTEGER;       {start entry number}
                    csCount: INTEGER;       {count number}
                END;
VDGamRecPtr = ^VDGammaRecord;
VDGammaRecord = RECORD
                    csGTable: ptr;          {pointer to gamma table (see Graphics Devices
                                             chapter in Inside Macintosh, Volume V)}
                END;
VDPgInfoPtr = ^VDPgInfo;
VDPgInfo = RECORD
                csMode: INTEGER;            {mode within device}
                csData: LONGINT;            {data supplied by driver}
                csPage: INTEGER;            {page to switch in}
                csBaseAddr: Ptr;            {base address of page}
            END;
```

Slot information applicable to the card associated with your video driver is contained in the device control entry, as described in the Device Manager chapter of *Inside Macintosh*, Volume V.

Control routines

The Macintosh II Operating System uses control calls to your video driver to set the video card to different configurations. Configuration changes might include choosing a different number of bits per pixel, changing the color table, or switching to a different video page.

Video driver routines that respond to these control calls are described in this section. The calls that all drivers must support are so identified; others are optional, and may return a NoErr code.

csCode = 0	csParam	= VDPgInfoPtr	[Init]
←	csMode	mode selected	[word]
←	csPage	page after reset	[word]
←	csBaseAddr	base address of video RAM	[long]

This required control routine must reset the video card to its startup state. The startup state of a video card should be one bit per pixel, with the default colors (if colors are supported) set to black and white. If the card supports multiple video pages in the default mode, page 0 should be switched in.

Your driver should also initialize its private storage areas, including areas for returned parameters.

```
csCode = 1                                              [KillIO]
```

This required control routine must stop any I/O requests currently being processed and remove any pending I/O requests. For most video cards, no change on the card is required. If the card does not support asynchronous calls, this routine may return a NoErr code.

```
csCode = 2      csParam    = VDPgInfoPtr                [SetMode]
        →       csMode       mode within device         [word]
        →       csPage       desired display page       [word]
        ←       csBaseAddr   base address of video RAM   [long]
```

This required control routine changes the card's video mode. The csMode parameter together with the csData parameter indicate the desired mode. The csData field is driver-dependent data supplied by an extension to the usual mode selection routines. Page numbers start with 0.

❖ *Note:* A video card may have a single mode and one video page. Because its available modes are listed in its declaration ROM, such a card would presumably never receive this call.

Color QuickDraw stores the current video mode in the slot's parameter RAM, and restores it when executing a Reset routine.

```
csCode = 3      csParam    = VDEntRecPtr                [SetEntries]
        →       csTable      pointer to color table     [long]
        →       csStart      first entry in table       [word]
        →       csCount      number of entries to set   [word]
```

This optional control routine should change the contents of the card's color look-up table, if any. If the card does not have a look-up table, it will never receive this call.

If the value of csStart is 0 or positive, the routine must install csCount entries starting at that position. If it is –1, the routine must access the contents of the Value fields in the csTable to determine which entries are to be changed. Both csStart and csCount are zero-based; their values are one less than the desired amount. For a description of the structure of a color look-up table, see the Color QuickDraw chapter of *Inside Macintosh,* Volume V.

❖ *Note:* The csStart value refers to logical position, not physical position. In four bits per pixel mode, for example, csStart values will still run 0,1,2,..., even though physical card registers 0,15,31,... are changed.

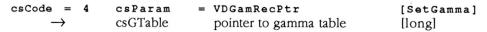

csCode	=	4	csParam	= VDGamRecPtr	[SetGamma]
→			csGTable	pointer to gamma table	[long]

This optional control routine creates a **gamma table** in the driver that corrects RGB color values. The gamma table compensates for nonlinearities in a display's color response by providing either a function or a look-up value that associates each displayed color with an absolute RGB value. It is used by the control routine with csCode = 3 (SetEntries) to modify the card's color look-up table. The gamma table is described in the chapter "Graphics Devices" of *Inside Macintosh,* Volume V.

Displays that do not use gamma-table correction tend to look over-saturated and dark. Although determining the correct values for a gamma table can be difficult without special tools, the table's contribution to image quality can be striking.

csCode	=	5	csParam	= VDPgInfoPtr	[GrayScreen]
→			csPage	pointer to video page	[long]

This optional control routine should fill the specified video page with a dithered gray pattern in the current video mode.

The purpose of this routine is to eliminate visual artifacts on the screen during mode changes. When an application changes the video card to a new mode, the contents of the video frame buffer will immediately acquire a new color meaning. To avoid annoying color flashes, the system uses this routine to set the entire color look-up table to a uniform shade of gray, before refilling the color look-up table with colors appropriate to the new mode.

csCode	=	6	csParam	= VDPgInfoPtr	[SetGray]
→			csMode	mode value	[word]

This optional control routine should determine whether the control routine with csCode = 3 (SetEntries) fills a card's color look-up table with actual colors or with the luminance-equivalent gray tones. For actual colors (the default case), the control routine is passed a csMode value of 0; for gray tones it is passed a csMode value of 1.

Luminance-equivalence should be determined by converting each RGB value into the hue-saturation-brightness system and then selecting a gray value of equal brightness. Mapping colors to luminance-equivalent gray tones lets a color monitor emulate a monochrome monitor exactly.

Status routines

The Macintosh II Operating System uses status calls to your video driver to determine the current configuration of the video card.

Video driver routines that respond to these calls are described in this section. The driver need process only pertinent status calls; others it can return with a status error.

csCode = 2	csParam	= VDPgInfoPtr	[GetMode]
←	csMode	mode within device	[word]
←	csPage	display page	[word]
←	csBaseAddr	base address of video RAM	[long]

This required status routine must return the current video mode, page, and base address.

csCode = 3	csParam	= VDEntRecPtr	[GetEntries]
↔	csTable	color table data	[long]
→	csStart	first entry in table	[word]
→	csCount	number of entries to set	[word]

This required status routine must return the specified number of consecutive color look-up table entries, starting with the specified first entry. If gamma-table correction is used, the values returned may not be the same as the values originally passed by SetEntries. If the value of csStart is 0 or positive, the routine must return csCount entries starting at that position. If it is −1, the routine must access the contents of the Value fields in the csTable to determine which entries are to be returned. Both csStart and csCount are zero-based; their values are one less than the desired amount.

csCode = 4	csParam	= VDPgInfoPtr	[GetPages]
←	csPage	number of pages	[word]
→	csMode	mode within device	[word]

This required status routine must return the total number of video pages available in the current video card mode (not the current page number).

csCode = 5	csParam	= VDPgInfoPtr	[GetBaseAddr]
→	csPage	desired page	[word]
←	csBaseAddr	base address of that page	[long]

This required status routine must return the base address of a specified page in the current mode. This allows video pages to be written to even when not displayed.

csCode = 6	csParam	= VDPgInfoPtr	[GetGray]
←	csMode	mode within device	[word]

This required status routine must return a value indicating whether the SetEntries routine has been conditioned to fill a card's color look-up table with actual colors or with the luminance-equivalent gray tones. For actual colors (the default case), the value returned by csMode is 0; for gray tones it is 1. The value returned can be set by a control call with csCode = 6.

Video driver example

Here is an example of a possible video card driver, written in the Macintosh Programmer's Workshop assembly language:

```
;===================================================================================

;General directives

                BLANKS          ON
                STRING          ASIS


;===================================================================================
;                       Local Vars, definitions, etc....
;===================================================================================


;This is device storage, a handle to which is stored in the dCtlStorage field of the DCE.

DCEPtr          EQU             0                       ;pointer to our DCE
saveMode        EQU             DCEPtr+4                ;the current mode setting
savePage        EQU             saveMode+2              ;the current page setting
saveBaseAddr    EQU             savePage+2              ;the current base address
saveSQElPtr     EQU             saveBaseAddr+4          ;the SQ element pointer (for
                                                        ;_SIntRemove)
GammaPtr        EQU             saveSQElPtr+4           ;the pointer to the gamma
                                                        ;correction table
GFlags          EQU             GammaPtr+4              ;flags word
dCtlSize        EQU             GFlags                  ;size of dCtlStorage

;Flags within GFlags word

GrayFlag        EQU             15                      ;luminance mapped if
                                                        ;GFlags(GrayFlag) = 1


;===================================================================================
;                       Video Driver Header
;===================================================================================

VidDrvr         DC.W            $4C00                   ;ctl,status,needsLock
                DC.W            0,0,0                   ;not an ornament

;Entry point offset table

                DC.W            VideoOpen-VidDrvr       ;open routine
                DC.W            VidDrvr-VidDrvr         ;no prime
                DC.W            VideoCtl-VidDrvr        ;control
                DC.W            VideoStatus-VidDrvr     ;status
                DC.W            VideoClose-VidDrvr      ;close

                STRING          Pascal
VideoTitle      DC.B            '.Display_Video_Sample'
                STRING          ASIS
                ALIGN           2                       ;make sure we're aligned
                DC.W            0                       ;version-0
```

```
;===============================================================================
;VideoOpen allocates private storage for the device in the DCE and locks
;       it down for perpetuity. It installs the interrupt handler and enables
;       the interrupts. It also sets the default gamma table included in the driver.
;
;Entry:         A0 = param block pointer
;               A1 = DCE pointer
;
;Locals:        A2 = Saved param block pointer
;               A3 = Saved DCE pointer
;               A4 = Saved interrupt handler ptr
;===============================================================================

;Save registers
VideoOpen       MOVE.L          A0,A2                   ;A2 <- param block pointer
                MOVE.L          A1,A3                   ;A3 <- DCE pointer

;Allocate private storage
                MOVEQ           #dCtlSize,D0            ;get size of parameters
                _ResrvMem       ,SYS                    ;make room as low as possible
                MOVEQ           #dCtlSize,D0            ;get size of parameters
                _NewHandle      ,SYS,CLEAR              ;get some memory for private
                                                        ; storage
                BNE             OpError                 ;=> return an error in open
                MOVE.L          A0,dCtlStorage(A3)      ;save returned handle in DCE
                _HLock                                  ;and lock it down

;Get and install the interrupt handler
                LEA             BeginIH,A4              ;Save pointer to interrupt
                                                        ; handler
                MOVEQ           #SQSize,D0              ;allocate a slot queue element
                _NewPtr         ,SYS,CLEAR              ;get it from system heap cleared
                BNE             OpError
                MOVE.W          #SIQType,SQType(A0)     ;setup queue ID
                MOVE.L          A4,SQAddr(A0)           ;setup int routine address
                MOVE.L          dctlDevBase(A3),SQParm(A0) ;save slot base addr as A3 parm
                CLR.L           D0
                MOVE.B          dctlSlot(A3),D0         ;setup slot #
                _SIntInstall                            ;and do install
                BNE.S           OpError

;Save SQElPtr for removal
                MOVE.L          dCtlStorage(A3),A1      ;Get pointer to private storage
                MOVE.L          (A1),A1
                MOVE.L          A0,saveSQElPtr(A1)      ;Save the SQ element pointer

;Enable interrupts
                ADD.L           #ClrVInt,A0             ;bump to interrupt reg
                CLR.B           (A0)                    ;clear it.

                MOVEQ           #0,D0                   ;no error
                BRA.S           EndOpen
;Error
OpError         MOVE.L          #OpenErr,D0             ;say can't open driver
EndOpen         RTS                                     ;return
```

```
;----------------------------------------------------------------------------
;                    The interrupt handler for the board
;----------------------------------------------------------------------------

;On entry A1 contains the slot base address
;D0-D3/A0-A3 have been preserved.

BeginIH         MOVE.L          A1,A0                   ;get screen base
                MOVE.L          A1,D0                   ;and save for later
                ADD.L           #ClrVInt,A0             ;get offset to register
                CLR.B           (A0)                    ;clear interrupt from card

                                                        ;D0 = $Fsxxxxxx
                ROL.L           #8,D0                   ;D0 <- $xxxxxxFs    Convert the
                                                        ;                   address into
                AND             #$0F,D0                 ;D0 <- $xxxx000s    the slot
                                                        ;                   number

                MOVE.L          JVBLTask,A0             ;call the VBL task manager
                JSR             (A0)                    ;with slot # in D0

                MOVEQ           #1,D0                   ;signal that int was serviced
                RTS                                     ;and return to caller

;============================================================================
;
;VideoClose releases the device's private storage.
;
;Entry:         A0 = param block pointer
;               A1 = DCE pointer
;
;Locals:        A2 = Saved param block pointer
;               A3 = Saved DCE pointer
;               A4 = Temporary
;
;============================================================================

VideoClose
                MOVE.L          A0,A2                   ;A2 <- param block pointer
                MOVE.L          A1,A3                   ;A3 <- DCE pointer

                MOVE.L          dCtlDevBase(A3),A4      ;A4 <- base address of device.
                ADD.L           #DisableVInt,A4         ;Adjust the base
                CLR.B           (A4)                    ;Disable interrupt from card

                MOVE.L          dCtlStorage(A3),A0      ;Get pointer to private storage
                MOVE.L          (A0),A0
                MOVE.L          saveSQElPtr(A0),A0      ;Get the SQ element pointer
                _SIntRemove                             ;Remove the interrupt handler
                MOVE.L          dCtlStorage(A3),A0      ;Dispose of the private storage
                _DisposHandle
                MOVEQ           #0,D0                   ;get error into D0
                RTS                                     ;return to caller
```

```
;==============================================================================
;
;Video Driver Control Call Handler.  Right now there are three calls:
;
;       (0)   Reset (VAR mode, page: INTEGER;VAR BaseAddr: Ptr);
;       (1)   KillIO
;       (2)   SetMode(mode, page: INTEGER;VAR BaseAddr: Ptr);
;
;       Entry: A0      = param block pointer
;              A1      = DCE pointer
;       Uses:  A2      = cs parameters (ie. A2 <- csParam(A0))  (must be preserved)
;              A3      = scratch (doesn't need to be preserved)
;              A4      = scratch (must be preserved)
;              D0-D3   = scratch (don't need to be preserved)
;
;       Exit:  D0              = error code
;
;==============================================================================

;Decode the call
VideoCtl      MOVEM.L     A0/A4/D4,-(SP)          ;save work registers (A0 is saved
                                                  ;because it is used by ExitDrvr)
              MOVE.W      csCode(A0),D0           ;get the opCode
              MOVE.L      csParam(A0),A2          ;A2 <- Ptr to control parameters

              CMP.W       #2,D0                   ;IF csCode NOT IN [0..2] THEN
              BHI.S       CtlBad                  ;Error, csCode out of bounds.
              LSL.W       #1,D0                   ;Adjust csCode to be an index into
                                                  ;the table
              MOVE.W      CtlJumpTbl(PC,D0.W),D0  ;Get the relative offset to the
                                                  ;routine
              JMP         CtlJumpTbl(PC,D0.W)     ;GOTO the proper routine.

CtlJumpTbl    DC.W        VidReset-CtlJumpTbl     ;$00 => VidReset
              DC.W        CtlGood-CtlJumpTbl      ;$01 => CtlGood
              DC.W        SetVidMode-CtlJumpTbl   ;$02 => SetVidMode

CtlBad        MOVEQ       #controlErr,D0          ;else say we don't do this one
              BRA.S       CtlDone                 ;and return

CtlGood       MOVEQ       #noErr,D0               ;return no error

CtlDone       MOVEM.L     (SP)+,A0/A4/D4          ;restore registers.
              BRA         ExitDrvr
```

```
VidReset
;---------------------------------------------------------------------------
;       Reset the card to its default (one bit per pixel)
;---------------------------------------------------------------------------

                BSR             TFBInit                             ;initialize the card
                MOVE            #OneBitMode,csMode(A2)              ;return default mode
                MOVE            #1,D1                               ;get depth in D1
                MOVEQ           #0,D0                               ;get page in D0
                MOVE            D0,csPage(A2)                       ;return the page
                MOVE.L          dCtlStorage(A1),A3                  ;get handle to our data
                MOVE.L          (A3),A3                             ;A3 = our data
                BSR             TFBSetDepth                         ;set the depth from D1
                BSR             TFBSetPage                          ;set the page from D0
                MOVE.L          saveBaseAddr(A3),csBaseAddr(A2)     ;return the base address
                BSR             GrayScreen                          ;paint the screen gray
                BRA.S           CtlGood                             ;=> no error

SetVidMode
;---------------------------------------------------------------------------
;       Set the card to the specified mode and page.
;       If either is invalid, returns badMode error.
;
;       If the card is already set to the specified mode, then do nothing.
;
;       Note: Mode set is [1,2,4,8].
;---------------------------------------------------------------------------

                MOVE.W          csMode(A2),D1       ;D1 = mode
                BSR             ChkMode             ;get mode, check, map to depth
                                                    ;(1, 2, 4 or 8)
                                                    ;{D1 <- depth}
                BNE.S           CtlBad              ;=> not a valid mode

                MOVE.W          csPage(A2),D0       ;D0 = page
                BSR             ChkPage             ;check page
                BNE.S           CtlBad              ;=> not a valid page

;Only set the mode if it has changed
;TFBSetDepth and TFBSetPage update the saved data in the dCtlStorage

SetEm           MOVE.L          dCtlStorage(A1),A3  ;get handle to our data
                MOVE.L          (A3),A3             ;A3 = our data
                MOVE.W          csMode(A2),D2       ;D2 = mode
                CMP             saveMode(A3),D2     ;has the mode changed?
                BEQ.S           ModeOK1             ;=> no, check the page
                BSR             TFBSetDepth         ;set the depth, get rowbytes
                BSR             TFBSetPage          ;set the page
                BRA.S           NoChange            ;=> and return

ModeOK1BSR      TFB             SetPage             ;set the page

NoChange        MOVE.L          saveBaseAddr(A3),csBaseAddr(A2)     ;return the base address
                BRA.S           CtlGood                             ;=> return no error
```

```
;================================================================================
;
;Video Driver Status Call Handler.  Right now there are three calls:
;
;        (2)   GetMode
;        (4)   GetPage
;        (5)   GetPageBase
;
;        Entry: A0    = param block
;               A1    = DCE pointer
;        Uses:  A2    = cs parameters (ie. A2 <- csParam(A0))   (must be preserved)
;               A3    = scratch (doesn't need to be preserved)
;               D0-D3 = scratch (don't need to be preserved)
;
;        Exit:  D0    = error code
;
;================================================================================

VideoStatus     MOVE.W       csCode(A0),D0                    ;get the opCode
                MOVE.L       csParam(A0),A2                   ;A2 <- Ptr to control parameters

                CMP.W        #5,D0                            ;IF csCode NOT IN [0..5] THEN
                BHI.S        StatBad                          ;Error, csCode out of bounds.
                LSL.W        #1,D0                            ;Adjust csCode to be an index into
                                                             ;the table
                MOVE.W       StatJumpTbl(PC,D0.W),D0          ;Get the relative offset to the
                                                             ;routine
                JMP          StatJumpTbl(PC,D0.W)             ;GOTO the proper routine.

StatJumpTbl     DC.W         StatBad-StatJumpTbl              ;$00 => Error
                DC.W         StatBad-StatJumpTbl              ;$01 => Error
                DC.W         GetMode-StatJumpTbl              ;$02 => GetMode
                DC.W         StatBad-StatJumpTbl              ;$03 => Error
                DC.W         GetPage-StatJumpTbl              ;$04 => GetPage
                DC.W         GetPageBase-StatJumpTbl          ;$05 => GetPageBase

StatBad         MOVEQ        #statusErr,D0                    ;else say we don't do this one
                BRA          ExitDrvr                         ;and return

StatGood        MOVEQ        #noErr,D0                        ;return no error
                BRA          ExitDrvr

GetMode
;--------------------------------------------------------------------------------
;                    Return the current mode
;--------------------------------------------------------------------------------

                MOVE.L       dCtlStorage(A1),A3               ;get handle to our storage
                MOVE.L       (A3),A3                          ;get pointer to our storage
                MOVE.W       saveMode(A3),csMode(A2)          ;return the mode
                MOVE.W       savePage(A3),csPage(A2)          ;return the page number
                MOVE.L       saveBaseAddr(A3),csBaseAddr(A2)  ;and the base address

                BRA.S        StatGood                         ;=> return no error
```

Video driver example   9-23

```
GetPage
;-----------------------------------------------------------------------------
;       Return the number of pages in the specified mode
;-----------------------------------------------------------------------------

                MOVE            csMode(A2),D1           ;get the mode
ChkMode                                                 ;check mode, get depth in D1
                BNE             StatBad                 ;=> not a valid mode
                MOVEQ           #5,D0                   ;512K vRAM: 5 pages
                MOVE            D0,csPage(A2)           ;return page count
                BRA             StatGood                ;=> return no error


GetPageBase
;-----------------------------------------------------------------------------
;       Return the base address for the specified page in the current mode
;-----------------------------------------------------------------------------

                MOVE.L          dCtlStorage(A1),A3      ;get handle to our storage
                MOVE.L          (A3),A3                 ;get pointer to our storage
                MOVE            saveMode(A3),D1         ;get the current mode
                BSR             ChkMode                 ;convert to depth in D1
                MOVE.W          csPage(A2),D0           ;get the requested page
                BSR             ChkPage                 ;is the page valid?
                BNE             StatBad                 ;=> no, just return

                MOVE            saveMode(A3),D1         ;get the current mode
                SUB             #OneBitMode,D1          ;make it 0 based
                LEA             ModeTbl,A0              ;point to tables
                MULU            4(A0,D1*8),D0           ;calc page * rowBytes
                MULU            6(A0,D1*8),D0           ;calc page * rowBytes * height
                ADD.L           defMBaseOffset,D0       ;which doesn't use first long
                ADD.L           dCtlDevBase(A1),D0      ;add base address for card
                MOVE.L          D0,csBaseAddr(A2)       ;return the base address

                BRA             StatGood                ;=> return no error


;-----------------------------------------------------------------------------
;       Exit from control or status.
;-----------------------------------------------------------------------------

ExitDrvr        BTST            #NoQueueBit,ioTrap(A0)  ;no queue bit set?
                BEQ.S           GoIODone                ;=> no, not immediate
                RTS                                     ;otherwise, it was an immediate call

GoIODone        MOVE.L          JIODone,A0              ;get the IODone address
                JMP             (A0)                    ;invoke it
```

```
;==============================================================================
;
;       Utilities (Hardware dependent)
;
;==============================================================================

TFBInit       RTS                                         ;Initialize the TFB

TFBSetDepth   RTS                                         ;Set the depth.

TFBSetPage    RTS                                         ;Set the page.

ChkMode       RTS                                         ;Check the current mode.

ChkPage       RTS                                         ;Check the current page.

GrayScreen    RTS                                         ;Gray the screen.

ModeTbl       DC.W    $AAAA,$AAAA,$0080,$01E0             ;one bit per pixel
              DC.W    $CCCC,$CCCC,$0100,$01E0             ;two bits per pixel
              DC.W    $F0F0,$F0F0,$0200,$01E0             ;four bits per pixel
              DC.W    $FF00,$FF00,$0400,$01E0             ;eight bits per pixel

                      END
```

Summary

Data types

```
TYPE

VDEntRecPtr = ^VDEntryRecord;
VDEntryRecord = RECORD
                 csTable: Ptr;           {pointer to color lookup table}
                  csStart: INTEGER;      {start entry number}
                  csCount: INTEGER;      {count number}
               END;
VDGamRecPtr = ^VDGammaRecord
VDGammaRecord = RECORD
                  csGTable: ptr;         {pointer to gamma table (see graphics devices
                                         chapter in Inside Macintosh, Volume V)}

               END;
VDPgInfoPtr = ^VDPgInfo;
VDPgInfo = RECORD
             csMode: INTEGER;            {mode within device}
             csData: LONGINT;            {data supplied by driver}
             csPage: INTEGER;            {page to switch in}
             csBaseAddr: Ptr             {base address of page}
          END;
```

Interrupt queue routines

```
FUNCTION SIntInstall(sIntQElemPtr: SQElemPtr; theSlot: INTEGER): OsErr;
FUNCTION SIntRemove(sIntQElemPtr: SQElemPtr; theSlot: INTEGER): OsErr;
```

Advanced control routines

csCode	csParam	Effect
0	VDPgInfoPtr	Resets card to startup state
1		Stops and purges I/O requests
2	VDPgInfoPtr	Changes card's video mode
3	VDEntRecPtr	Changes card's color table (if any)
4	VDGamRecPtr	Creates a gamma table
5	VDPgInfoPtr	Fills video page with gray
6	VDPgInfoPtr	Selects actual colors or luminance-equivalent gray tones

Advanced status routines

csCode	csParam	Effect
2	VDPgInfoPtr	Returns card's current video mode, page, and base address
3	VDEntRecPtr	Returns color table entries
4	VDPgInfoPtr	Returns number of video pages available
5	VDPgInfoPtr	Returns base address of specified page
6	VDPgInfoPtr	Returns selection status of actual colors or luminance-equivalent gray tones

Assembly-language information

Data structures

```
;Use with control and status calls where csCode = 3
csFirst      EQU    0              ;[word] first color table entry
csCount      EQU    csFirst+2      ;[word] number of entries to set
csTable      EQU    csCount+2      ;[long] pointer to color table
                                   ;entry = value, r, g, b : INTEGER
;Use with control calls where csCode = 0, 2, 5, or 6
;and with status calls where csCode = 2, 4, 5, or 6
csMode       EQU    0              ;[word] mode within device
csData       EQU    csMode+2       ;[long] data supplied by driver
csPage       EQU    csData+4       ;[word] page to switch in
csBaseAddr   EQU    csPage+2       ;[long] base address of page
```

Interrupt queue routines

```
;To install a new queue element
        LEA         PollRoutine,A1        ;Get routine address
        MOVE.L      A1,SQAddr(A0)         ;Set address
        MOVE.W      Prio,SQPrio(A0)       ;Set priority
        MOVE.L      A1Parm, SQParm(A0)    ;Save A1 parameter
        MOVE.W      Slot,D0               ;Set slot number
        _SIntInstall                      ;Do installation

;To remove a queue element
        LEA         MySQEl,A0             ;Pointer to queue element
        _SIntRemove                       ;Remove it
```

Chapter 10

NuBus Design Examples

This chapter contains performance-proven examples of design for the Apple implementation of the NuBus interface in the Macintosh II.

NuBus Test Card

The NuBus Test Card (NTC) is an example of a complete master/slave NuBus slot card. In use, this card allows the Macintosh II central processor (or other NuBus master card) to test the functionality of the NuBus slave and master response logic. It provides an example of the type of logic necessary to implement a NuBus master card.

This description is to assist a hardware engineer who wants to see how a typical NuBus card is designed. No motivation for the design choices is given. It is intended as a description of an existing design and it is assumed that the reader is familiar with NuBus, PALs, and so forth.

Overview of operation

The NTC in slave mode is addressed by the MC68020 on the main logic board (or any bus master) and properly written, so that the three NTC registers then contain the information needed for the following step. The MC68020 next addresses one of the registers to seek bus mastership; the NTC waits a programmed number of clock cycles and then arbitrates to become bus master. When it becomes bus master the NTC accomplishes the read or write to an address that was stored in an address register in the previous step.

Programming model (registers)

This section describes how the NTC looks to a programmer.

The NTC provides three registers (Address, Data, and Master). The three registers can be accessed by addressing the NTC as a *slave*. The first two registers (Address and Data) can be read from and written to; they support only NuBus word (32-bit) operations. Both of these registers can be used to test the basic data paths of the bus. However, these registers are primarily intended to supply the address and data that will be used during the NTC's master transaction, when the NTC becomes bus *master*.

The 11-bit Master register is write only. When the Master register is written to, the NTC will (after a programmed delay) initiate a transaction in which it becomes the bus master. The bits of the value written to the Master register are interpreted as shown in Table 10-1.

Bits 10 and 9 contain the TM1 and TM0 values that (along with address bits AD1 and AD0) define the transfer mode of the master transaction (see Table 3-1, "Transfer Mode Coding"). Bits 7 through 0 contain the programmed time delay (in 1's complement form).

Table 10-1
Master register interpretation

Bit	Assigned meaning
D11	TM1 value (1 means /TM1 is asserted [low]), essentially the Read/Write indicator
D10	TM0 value (1 means /TM0 is asserted [low]), essentially the data item length indicator
D9	Lock bit (1 means execute a locked transaction)
D8	0 (zero)
D7–D0	A 1's complement Delay value

The master cycle is delayed, after the execution of the write to the Master register, by the number of clock periods specified by Delay. Delay is the value in the least significant eight bits of the Master register; that value is incremented to $FF before the NTC becomes bus master and initiates a transaction.

The register addresses are given in Table 10-2; s is the number of the slot into which the card is inserted.

Table 10-2
Register addresses

Address	Name
$Fss8 0000	Master (write-only) register
$Fss0 0000	Address register
$Fss4 0000	Data register

Byte swapping and the NTC

Byte swapping is necessary when interacting with the NTC because of the design of the NTC, the re-ordering of bytes when the Macintosh II transfers data across the NuBus, and the byte ordering of the NuBus.

As noted in Chapter 4, the Macintosh II NuBus interface (BIU) performs a byte swapping of data values (see Figure 4-2 and the BIU in Figures 1-1 and 1-3). For example, the byte containing bits D31–D24 of the MC68020 (referred to as byte 0), is swapped so that the byte is transferred to NuBus byte lane 0 (/AD7–/AD0). This preserves byte address consistency between cards on the NuBus. Every NuBus interface must be designed so that its byte 0 is placed on NuBus byte lane 0, byte 1 on byte lane 1, and so forth. If you transfer a MC68020 word of $0011 2233 to the NuBus, then, on the NuBus, it would appear as $3322 1100 (assuming that we display the bytes as most significant byte (MSB) to least significant byte (LSB) in left-to-right order).

As can be seen on the schematic for the NTC (Figure 10-1), the Address and Data registers are connected so that a byte written to a given NuBus byte lane will be placed back on the same byte lane when these registers are read from as a slave or when driven to as a master. That is, there is no byte swapping performed by the NTC itself.

This design of the NTC has ramifications in how the values are written to its registers. For example, an Address register value must be byte swapped when written from the MC68020. For example, if we want the NTC to make a transaction to $1122 3344 (in NuBus format), we must write the data so that the MSB of the Address register contains the $11 byte; this means that NuBus byte lane 3 must contain the $11. However, because NuBus byte lane 3 is driven by MC68020 byte 3, the value we write must have the $11 in the LSB of the MC68020 value (where byte 3 belongs). Following this logic for the rest of the bytes, it should be apparent that the appropriate value to be written by the MC68020 to the NTC Address register is $4433 2211.

The same byte swapping must be done to values that are written to the Data register in preparation for a NuBus write by the NTC. Remember, however, that data values that are to reference the Macintosh II main logic board (for example, RAM) are byte swapped by the BIU as the transaction is made. Thus, data values that are destined for (or read from) Macintosh II RAM will not look byte swapped. For example, suppose that we set up the NTC to read a Macintosh II RAM location that contains $1234 5678 (MC68020 form). When we read the Data register after the transaction completes, we read $1234 5678! The reason is that when the NTC did the read, the BIU placed the data onto NuBus as $7856 3412 (due to the byte swapping of the BIU). Then, when we read the Data register, the value is byte swapped by the BIU (again!) so that the MC68020 sees the value as $1234 5678. If we wanted a *NuBus* value of $1234 5678, then the appropriate MC68020 value would be $7856 3412.

It is important to make a clear distinction of whether a value is specified as viewed from the perspective of the Macintosh II processor or the NuBus interface. NuBus referenced values need to be byte swapped in Macintosh II terms; Macintosh II referenced values do not.

Programming the NTC

In the following discussions, values for various NuBus fields are specified. In all cases, the values are the logical value; remember that these are the complement of the NuBus signals. For example, if TM1 is a 1, then that implies that /TM1 (the NuBus signal) will be *low*. Also, all references to data width will be in NuBus terms; that is, NuBus word (32-bit), halfword, and byte.

To cause the NTC to perform a master cycle, the following two-step sequence must be performed:

1. The Address register is set up with the desired master transaction's address.

❖ *Note:* Because of the design of the NTC, the Address register must be written with a byte-swapped value. For example, a NuBus address of $1234 5678 must be byte-swapped to become $7856 3412. Furthermore, the lower two bits of the Address register become part of the NuBus transfer mode. The values of these two bits must be modified to correspond to the desired transfer mode encoding, not what a MC68020 program would use for the equivalent access. The examples given later in this section illustrate the byte swapping.

   If the master transaction is to be a *write,* then the Data register must be written with the data that will be transmitted when the NTC becomes bus master.

2. The Master register is written. The value must include the proper TM1–TM0, Lock , and Delay values. After the Master register has been written, the NTC will delay for the number of clock periods specified by Delay, and then make the master transaction.

Examples

This section describes two examples of setting up the NTC to execute master transactions. In these examples, references to the NuBus transfer mode will be given in the 4-bit form </TM1,/TM0,/AD1,/AD0>, where the bit values represent the corresponding NuBus signal level—H for high and L for low. Values of the Master register bits for AD1–AD0 and TM1–TM0 are the logical values (0/1). Remember that a 0 written to a register will be placed on the NuBus as an H (and a 1 as an L).

Word read of $0000 1234 (Macintosh II RAM): Suppose that we wish to cause the NTC to perform a word read transaction to location $1234; this causes a read of the Macintosh II RAM. The proper NuBus transfer mode for reading a NuBus word is <HHHH>, as shown in Table 3-1. Thus the values written to TM1–TM0 and AD1–AD0 are adjoined to form the 4-bit transfer mode code <0000>. Hence, the registers are written by the MC68020 as

$3412 0000 into Address
$0000 00FF into Master

This will cause the NTC to execute a word read (because TM1–TM0 and AD1–AD0 are all 0), from location 0 immediately (FF is the 1's complement of 00, for a Delay of zero clock periods).

Halfword 0 write (of $5678) to $F900 1234 (slot 9) after $40 clock cycles: The proper transfer mode value is <LHHL>, from Table 3-1. Therefore, the value for <TM1–TM0, AD1–AD0> is <1001> and the registers are programmed to be loaded as follows:

$3512 00F9 into Address
$7856 xxxx into Data
$0000 08BF into Master (D11–D8 in Table 10-1, binary 1000 is 8 in hex; $BF is the 1's
                complement of $40)

❖ *Note:* In the last nibble of $1234, $4 = 0100 in binary, so AD1 = 0 and AD0 = 0. But AD1 and AD0 must be changed to encode the least significant two bits of the transfer mode, so AD0 is changed to a 1 and now 0101 = $5. Then $F900 1235 becomes $3512 00F9 when byte swapped. The address $F900 1234 on the NuBus is obtained by writing $3512 00F9 into the Address register.

The Data register is written so that when the master transaction is performed, the data will be in the proper byte lanes. Halfword 0 data is contained in byte lanes 1 (MSB) and 0 (LSB). Hence, you need to write the data from the MC68020 such that the $56 (MSB) is in byte 1 and $78 (MSB) is in byte 0. The value $7856 xxxx is what must be written by the MC68020.

Hardware organization

This section describes the hardware used to mechanize the NuBus Test Card. The schematic is shown in Foldout 3 at the end of the book. PAL equations are displayed in Appendix A.

The NTC consists of

☐ 4 NuBus address/data buffers (74ALS651s), U1-U4 (also called transceivers)

☐ 8 octal latches (74ALS374s), U5-U12, which implement the Address and Data registers

☐ 1 ROM socket, U13, for the declaration ROM

☐ 2 4-bit counters (74ALS161s), U23-U24, which implement the Delay counter

☐ 1 74F86, U14, and 1 74F30, U15, which form an address comparator

☐ 5 PALs, U16-U20, which implement the control logic

☐ 1 74F04 inverter, U21

☐ 1 74F02 NOR, U22

NuBus address/data buffers

The NuBus address or data buffers, U1–U4, are grouped into two parts. U1 can be independently driven onto the NuBus, while U2–U4 are latched into the NTC. This allows the addresses for the ROM to be held during a ROM read cycle without additional parts. For all other operations, all of the buffers are either set for transferring data from or to the bus in unison.

Address and Data registers

The two sets of latches (U5–U8, U9–U12) form the Address and Data registers. They are latched during a write to the corresponding register and are enabled upon either a slave read to the register or during a master transaction.

Address comparison

U14 and U15 are wired so that the output of U15 is low when an address of $FSxx xxxx is present on the /AD lines. This signal is used by the SLAVE PAL to detect the start cycle to the card.

SLAVE PAL

The slave PAL (SLAVE PAL) is the state machine for slave accesses to the NTC. It also latches the state of AD19–AD18, which are used by other PALs.

ARB PAL

The arbitration PAL (ARB PAL) is responsible for performing the NuBus arbitration process. When /ARBCY is asserted, the /ID3–/ID0 value is used to drive the /ARB3–/ARB0 lines. However, when /ARB detects that a higher priority value is present on the /ARB3–/ARB0 lines, it removes drive from its lower priority lines, following the NuBus rules. The GRANT signal is asserted when /ARB recognizes that its /ARB3–/ARB0 value is valid; GRANT is used by the master PAL to detect that the NTC has won ownership of the bus.

MASTER PAL

The master PAL (MASTER PAL) is responsible for controlling a master transaction on the bus. It idles until it detects that both the MASTER and MASTERD (delayed MASTER) input signals are true. It will then go through a state sequence to perform the transaction. The master PAL can execute two types of transactions: normal and locked. The state sequence is slightly different for each case. See the timing diagram, Figure 10-2, for the sequences of each. Note that the diagram shows the shortest slave response. In actual use, most accesses hold in the wait state (DTACY asserted) while awaiting an /ACK for more than one cycle.

MISC PAL

The miscellaneous PAL (MISC PAL) is used to decode the state machine signals and drive oncard devices. The outputs control the gating of the 651's, 374's, and so forth.

NBDRVR PAL

The NuBus driver PAL (NBDRVR PAL) is responsible for driving all NuBus signals. As in the MISC PAL, NBDRVR decodes the state machine signals to determine the timing for these signals.

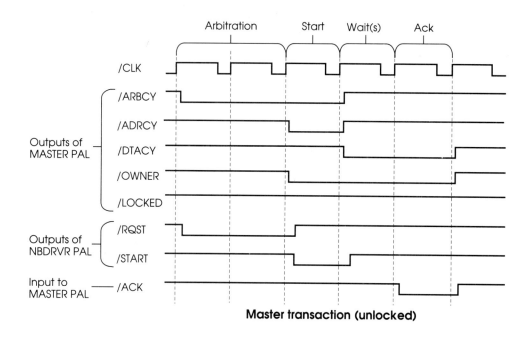

Master transaction (unlocked)

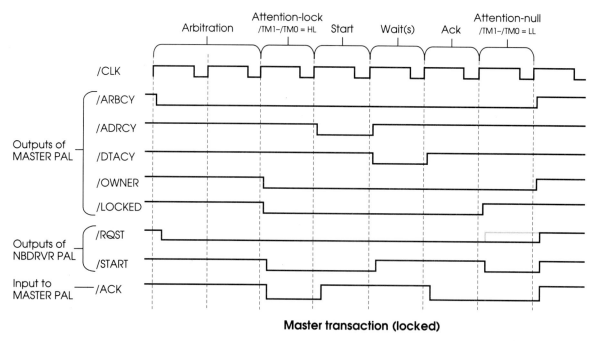

Master transaction (locked)

Figure 10-1
Master transaction timing, normal and locked

Slave operation

During a slave access by another master, the operation of the NTC is determined by the slave, miscellaneous, and NuBus driver PALs. The slave PAL determines that an access to the NTC is being made (by looking at the slot decode, /START, and /ACK) and performs timing. The miscellaneous PAL determines whether to clock (ACLK/DCLK) or output enable (AOE/DOE) the 374's, enable the appropriate 651 direction, and so forth, based upon the inputs from the slave PAL.

When the slave PAL detects that the Master register is being written, it will finish the slave access and also set its MASTER output. During the data cycle of the Master register write, the slave PAL latches the values of D11–D10, and causes the values of D7–D0 to be latched into the 161 counters. During the subsequent master transaction, the slave PAL will not respond until the /MSTDN signal is asserted.

Master operation

A master transaction is begun when the slave PAL sets the MASTER signal. After the 161's have counted up to $FF, the master PAL will begin the master state sequence.

After arbitration, it will do its start cycle and wait for the acknowledge cycle. When /ACK is detected, /MSTDN will be signaled; this will cause the slave PAL to start looking for new slave transactions to the NTC.

❖ *Note:* This design violates the letter of the law of NuBus in one regard; however, this violation causes no problem in a real system. The violation occurs at the end of a locked transaction. /RQST is held asserted during the final attention-null cycle; it should be released during that cycle. No problem exists because either the NTC is the last request (/RQST) or it is not. If it is the last, then the only effect is that new requestors must wait an additional clock cycle. If it is not the last, then /RQST would stay asserted anyway. In either case, the proper operation of the bus ensues.

SCSI-NuBus Test Card

This card is an example of how a simple, 8-bit I/O chip may be supported over NuBus.

The SCSI-NuBus Test Card allows the test of declaration ROM images, in particular, the Slot Manager. The card allows an image of a bootstrap program (contained in the card's declaration ROM) to boot the Macintosh II Operating System from an attached SCSI drive. In addition, the card provides a small RAM which is accessable in super slot space for the testing of 32-bit address mode switching.

The *ROM* is really a RAM which can be written at the assigned ROM address space. The RAM chip may be replaced with a real ROM when desired.

Software overview

The software model of this card is essentially the same as that of the SCSI chip on the main logic board, except that it is accessed via NuBus. The address offsets of the registers and pseudo-DMA are the same as on a Macintosh SE or Macintosh Plus.

The SCSI chip can generate NuBus interrupts (via /NMRQ) from both IRQ and DRQ; this interrupt can be disabled.

The declaration ROM is accessed at the top of the 1MB address space. The SCSI chip is accessed at the bottom of the space. The 8K of RAM is accessable only as a super slot. Note that all of the devices are connected to byte lane 3 (bits /AD31–AD24) of NuBus. They are thus addressed from the MC68020 as bytes at addresses with the least significant two bits equal to 3 (/AD1=/AD0=1, low). See Table 3-1, Figure 4-1, and the NuBus Test Card examples earlier in this chapter.

Hardware overview

This section describes the hardware components and how they function. Figure 10-3 is an electrical schematic of the SCSI-NuBus Test Card; Figure 10-4 is the timing diagram. The PAL equations are in Appendix B.

The function of each chip on the card is as follows.

NuBus transceivers (ALS651's)

Three 74ALS651's are used to implement the NuBus transceiver function.

One of them is the data transceiver; it connects to byte lane 3 (bits /AD31–/AD24) and serves to transmit and receive the byte-wide data over NuBus. During idle states, the data transceiver is also monitoring the bus to feed data into the slot decode logic.

Two 74ALS651's are used to latch addresses (/AD2–/AD14,/AD18,/AD19) and the write/read signal (/TM1) for the SCSI, ROM, and RAM accesses. These chips are clocked by a signal from stNUBUS2 every falling edge of /CLK until stNUBUS1 detects an access to the card. They then hold onto the low-order address bits that were present during the transaction's start cycle.

Slot Decode (F86/F30)

This card uses a combination of a 74F86 and a 74F30 to perform slot decoding. Two sets are used, one for the basic slot space decode ($Fsxx xxxx) and the second for the super slot access decode ($sxxx xxxx).

NuBus state machine (stNUBUS1 PAL)

This PAL (16R8B) performs the basic NuBus timing for the card. When either mySLOT or mySUPER is detected during a start cycle, the PAL generates /SLOT or /SUPER and starts a 2-bit counter (/S2, /S1), which is used by stMISC. The value of /TM1 during the start cycle is latched to form the /IOR signal, the assertion of which indicates a read.

NuBus signal generator (stNUBUS2 PAL)

This PAL (16L8B) decodes the state of /SLOT, /SUPER, and /S2 to generate the acknowledge cycle and control the latching of the 651's.

stNUBUS2 is also used to generate the open-collector /NMRQ signal for presentation of interrupts to the main logic board.

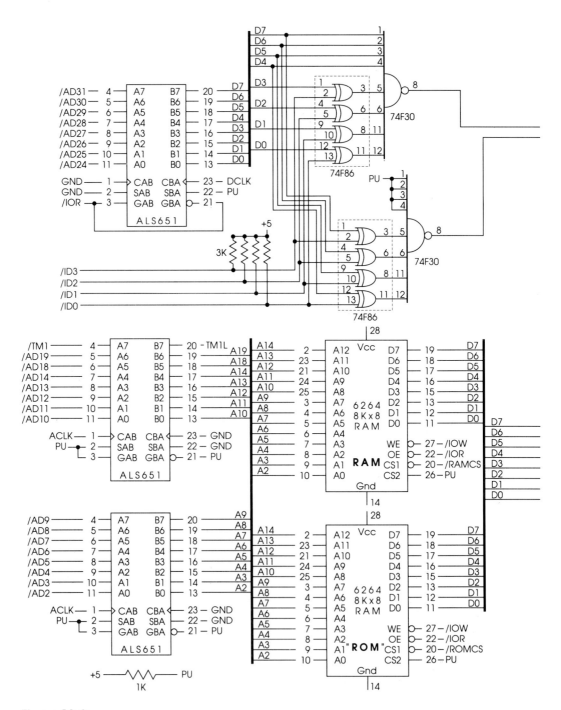

Figure 10-2
Schematic of SCSI-NuBus Test Card

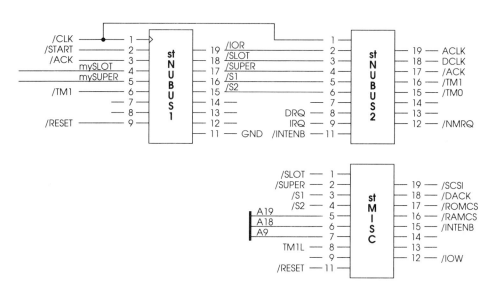

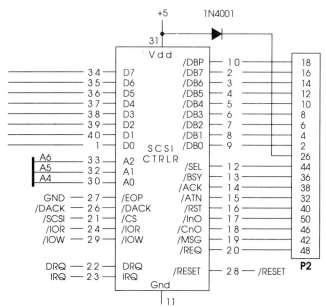

NOTE: All IC terminals and lines labeled Gnd
or GND are connected to power ground.

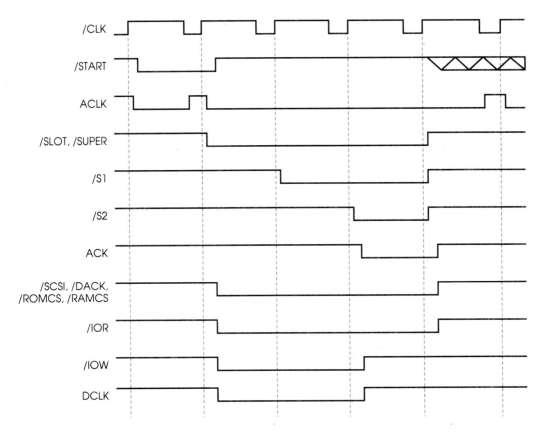

Figure 10-3
SCSI-NuBus timing diagram

Decode and timing (stMISC PAL)

This PAL (16L8B) generates the basic I/O strobes to the SCSI, ROM, and RAM. It uses the /SLOT and /SUPER signals in addition to the latched address bits to perform the decode.

The INTENB signal is a latch that controls the generation of /NMRQ. It is set by accessing a location of $Fsx 820x; it may be cleared by accessing $Fsx 800x.

SCSI chip (NCR5380)

This chip is identical to that used in the Macintosh Plus. It connects to a SCSI bus via the connector P2, which also supplies the TRMPWR signal for SCSI termination.

Pseudo-ROM

The *ROM* of this card was designed to allow software designers quick update capability. It is really an 8K x 8 RAM which can be written using the ROM address space. However, a real 8K x 8 ROM may be inserted instead.

RAM

The RAM chip is an 8K x 8 RAM which is accessible only by addressing super slot space

PAL descriptions

The source code of the three PALs is in Appendix B. Refer to these listings, along with the timing diagram and schematic, for a more detailed understanding of how the card works.

Design of a simple disk controller

This section describes the electrical and interface characteristics of a slave-only disk controller card that allows the Macintosh II computer to communicate with a generic disk drive through the NuBus.

The disk controller card plugs into any NuBus slot on the Macintosh II main logic board and connects to a floppy disk drive located outside the Macintosh II. The disk controller card consists of a disk controller IC and a disk interface IC, a sector buffer RAM, a declaration ROM, various address and data buffers, and three 24-pin PALs. All controlling firmware exists in the Macintosh II. The controller is memory mapped into a single NuBus slot space.

System configuration

The controller package consists of a disk controller card, a cable running from controller to disk drive, and a floppy disk drive. The disk controller card connects the disk drive to the Macintosh II central processor through one of the six slots on the Macintosh II main logic board. One end of the cable connects to the controller card and the two connectors on the other end of the cable connect to the disk drive.

Interface card block diagram

The controller card is made up of the following parts shown in Figure 10-5:

Address/data bus transceivers: These 74LS640-1's buffer the internal address/data bus of the controller from the NuBus address/data bus.

Address counters: These 74LS169 counters latch the RAM/ROM address from the NuBus during RAM/ROM reads or writes and count down the RAM address during DMA transfers to or from the disk.

RAM: This is the 2048 x 8 sector buffer RAM. Data to be transferred to or from the disk is placed here by the processor before disk transfers are initiated.

ROM: This is the NuBus declaration ROM. The NuBus Slot Manager accesses this ROM on power-up to determine the controller's type and modes of access.

Slot address decoder PAL: This PAL20L10 determines if the controller's slot address is selected. It uses the signal /START and address decoding to compare if the upper nibble of the address is an $F and if the address lines A24–A27 and D0–D3 compare with the hard-wired slot ID address.

State machine PAL: This PAL20X10 generates the timing for programmed I/O and internal DMA transfers on the controller.

State decoder PAL: The state number is decoded by this PAL to produce control signals needed by the various parts of the controller.

Control/status driver: The control driver places the signals /ACK, /TM0, and /TM1 on the NuBus at the end of a NuBus access of the controller. The status driver allows the following signals to be read by the processor: disk controller interrupt, internal operation pending, and disk in place.

Floppy disk controller IC: This LSI chip contains the circuitry necessary to communicate with the generic disk drive. Coupled with the companion disk interface IC chip, it handles all operations with the drive including reading and writing data, formatting, seeking, sensing drive status, and recalibrating.

Floppy disk interface IC: This chip provides drive and timing support to the disk controller IC. It contains write precompensation and phase-locked loop circuitry.

Disk interface driver: The disk interface driver buffers and provides current drive for several signals coming from and going to the disk drive. It also is used as a multiplexer for four signals: FLT/TR0, WP/TS, FR/STP, and LCT/DIR.

16-MHz crystal clock oscillator: This oscillator provides a 16-MHz clock to the disk interface IC for use in the drive interface.

NuBus

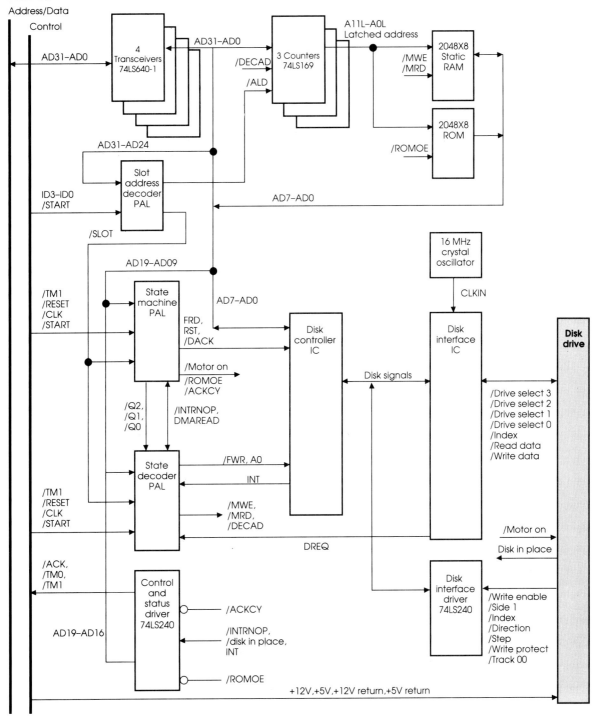

Figure 10-4
Floppy disk controller block diagram

Design of a simple disk controller   10-17

Floppy disk controller logic

The disk interface is provided by the disk controller IC, the disk interface IC, and two 74LS240 drivers. The disk controller IC is the controlling chip and communicates with the disk interface IC. Details of this logic are not directly relevant to design of NuBus interfaces and so they are not given here.

NuBus interface logic

The controller connects to NuBus via several drivers and PALs. The address/data bus is tied to four 74LS640-1 transceivers which invert each bit. Control signals such as /START, the slot identification bits /ID3–/ID0, and the mode bits TM1–TM0 are used to time data transfers to and from the NuBus. Status information is passed to the NuBus along with the control signal /ACK by the status driver (74LS240). DMA operations are controlled by the state machine and state machine decoder PALs.

Certain key signals are described in Table 10-3.

Table 10-3
RAM access signals

Signal name	Signal description
/SLOT	Signals that a NuBus cycle to the controller is active
/ALD	Used to load the RAM/ROM address into the address counters; gates the clock signal into the synchronous counters
/FWR	Enables disk controller IC write enable
/FRD	Enables disk controller IC read enable
A0	Disk controller IC register select: 0 selects main status register, 1 selects data register
SR	Direction signal to bidirectional driver on the address/data bus: 0 means write to NuBus, 1 means read from NuBus
/DREQ	Requests DMA cycle from disk controller IC or disk interface IC
/DACK	Acknowledges the DMA cycle requested
/ACKCY	Gates /ACK and the TM1–TM0 bits
/MWE	Enables RAM memory write
/MRD	Enables RAM memory read output
/INTRNOP	When asserted, indicates internal DMA operation in process
/DMAREAD	Indicates a DMA read operation when asserted
/DECAD	Enables the DMA address counters to decrement by one memory location

Programmed I/O (PIO) operations

Control and status information is passed to and from the controller using programmed I/O operations. PIO transfers include RAM and disk controller IC reads and writes, and ROM reads. The motor on and reset signals are asserted and deasserted using PIO operations. Refer to Figure 10-5.

A typical PIO transfer begins with the assertion of the signal /START. The slot address is valid during the time /START is asserted and is recognized by the slot decoder PAL. It asserts the signals /SLOT and /ALD. /SLOT indicates that the NuBus cycle is currently active. /ALD is used as a clock enable signal for loading the RAM or ROM address into the counters. /ALD is also used as a clock enable to latch /TM1 and address bits A19/D11, A18/D10, and A17/D9. These are later used to assert the signals /FRD, /FWR, /MWE, /MRD, SR, /ROMOE, and A0. The state machine, recognizing /SLOT, begins sequencing through a NuBus cycle, going to states 1, 3, and then 2. In state 2 it asserts /ACKCY, which in turn enables the status driver to assert the /TM1–/TM0 bits and /ACK. The signals /FRD, /FWR, /MWE, /MRD, SR, /ROMOE, and A0 are asserted or deasserted according to the address on the address/data bus during /START and the state number.

The signals /FRD, /FWR, and A0 are used to transfer data to and from the disk controller IC.

RAM accesses are controlled by /MWE and /MRD. The ROM is read when /ROMOE is active. The signal SR is used to control the direction of the 74LS640 transceivers.

On-card DMA operations

Transfers to and from the sector buffer RAM are done by on-card DMA. DMA is not done through the NuBus because this card is a slave only.

The state machine is placed in internal DMA mode by writing to an address in the range $FssC 0000 through $FssF FFFF. See the section "Memory Map and the Declaration ROM" for the rationale behind the ss in these addresses. DMA operations from the disk to RAM require that the last command word to the disk controller IC be written to a location in the range from $FssC 0000 through $FssD FFFF.

DMA operations from RAM to the disk require that the last command word to the disk controller IC be written to a location in the range from $FssE 0000 through $FssF FFFF.

After a DMA operation has been requested, transfers to or from the disk are then initiated and controlled internally. After an operation is complete, the controller interrupts the processor. The address bits A13–A2 are the beginning RAM memory location that the DMA operation uses. This address is decremented until it reaches zero and terminates the DMA operation.

An attempt to read or write to any address in the controller's address range during a DMA operation will be ignored, although the NuBus cycle is terminated with normal status.

When a DMA operation is requested, the signal /INTRNOP is asserted along with /DMAREAD if the operation is a DMA read. A /SLOT or a /DACK signal causes the state machine to begin sequencing. Because the /DACK signal holds off /SLOT, if both happen simultaneously, the DMA operation is first completed, then the NuBus cycle is acknowledged.

The signal /DACK occurs on the first rising edge of /CLK after the signal DREQ is asserted, and is held until the DMA cycle is complete. The disk controller IC/disk interface IC pair initiates the DMA cycle by asserting DREQ.

Memory map and the declaration ROM

The controller's device select space ranges from $Fss0 0000 to $FssF FFFF and is divided up into eight blocks. The designator ss is used to indicate the slot space where s is the slot number and ranges from $9 through $E in the Macintosh II machine.

Table 10-4 summarizes the address decodes.

Table 10-4
Device select decode addresses

Address range	Device selected and action resulting
$Fss0 0000–$Fss1 FFFF	Read status information from disk controller
$Fss2 0000–$Fss3 FFFF	Read or write control information to the disk controller
$Fss4 0000–$Fss5 FFFF	Begin internal DMA cycle reading data from disk
$Fss6 0000–$Fss7 FFFF	Begin internal DMA cycle writing data from disk
$Fss8 0000–$Fss9 FFFF	Enable RAM for reading or writing
$FssA 0000–$FssB FFFF	Reserved
$FssC 0000–$FssD FFFF	Turn drive motor on by writing; turn motor and controller's reset signal off by reading (Interrupts are enabled when the motor is on!)
$FssE 0000–$FssF FFFF	Access ROM by reading; turn controller's reset signal on by writing

It is through the data register that commands, data, and values in status registers 0–3 are passed. Any disk operation is initiated by passing the several commands required to the disk controller IC via this register. If a format, read data, read deleted data, write data, or write deleted data command is requested, the data or parameters required by the disk controller IC during its execution phase must have been previously loaded into the sector buffer RAM.

The final command code written to the disk controller IC is written via the DMA execute addressing space. The read track operation is not supported because the quantity of data transferred exceeds the sector buffer size. After the execute portion of an operation is completed, the disk controller IC may give back status information in status registers 0–3.

In order to read the status of the disk controller, an additional status register is provided. This register is accessed by a MOVE.W to the address space from $FssE 0000 through $FssF FFFF (ROM).

Chapter 11

The Macintosh II
Video Card

The Macintosh II Video Card is a high-performance color video card for use with the Macintosh II computer. The card provides variable-depth color graphics at up to 8 bits per pixel. The card contains a color look-up table (CLUT) with a 16.8 million color palette and an 8-bit digital-to-analog converter (DAC) for each of three channels (RGB).

Firmware support for the card is provided by the declaration ROM. The declaration ROM contains a low-level card driver that performs all of the interface and hardware management functions for the video card. The declaration ROM is described later in this chapter.

Operating System support, as exemplified by Color QuickDraw, the Color Manager, and the Slot Manager is detailed in *Inside Macintosh,* Volume V.

Functional operation

The video card controls the output of data to a video device through the use of the Frame Buffer Controller (FBC) and the color look-up table (CLUT). The declaration ROM firmware provides the interface between the card hardware and application software running on the Macintosh II processor.

Figure 11-1 is a block diagram of the video card. The following paragraphs describe the function of each of the blocks shown in Figure 11-1.

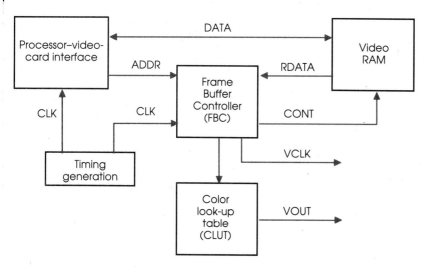

Figure 11-1
Video card block diagram

Processor–to–video card interface

The processor–to–video card interface is executed in both hardware and firmware. The hardware side is the standard NuBus electrical interface, described in Chapters 1 through 7.

The firmware side is implemented in the declaration ROM, described later in this chapter and in Chapter 8, "NuBus Card Firmware."

Timing generation

The timing generation circuitry on the video card generates these basic signals:

☐ the Frame Buffer Controller (FBC) interface signals

☐ the NuBus handshake and control signals

☐ other video card control signals

The timing generation circuitry provides three signals for the FBC interface:

☐ /PAS

☐ /RAMSEL

☐ a 20-MHz frame buffer clock

The /PAS signal acts as an address strobe to the FBC. Addresses from the NuBus are latched on the FBC at the falling edge of /PAS, and the FBC will not initiate a RAM cycle if /PAS is not active. /PAS remains active until /ACK is returned to the NuBus master.

The /RAMSEL signal indicates that a RAM bank has been selected and a RAM cycle will be initiated on the following NuBus clock. /RAMSEL serves to synchronize the FBC to the NuBus. The FBC will initiate a RAM cycle any time /RAMSEL and /PAS are active and a RAM refresh cycle is not being executed.

The 20-MHz frame buffer clock is generated from the 10-MHz NuBus clock via a 100 nanosecond tapped delay line. The 20-MHz clock, labeled *20M* on the timing diagrams, is the video card clock.

Frame Buffer Controller (FBC)

The **Frame Buffer Controller** is a register-controlled CMOS gate array. A set of 16 8-bit registers in the FBC is loaded with the parameters required by both the FBC and the declaration ROM. These registers are loaded during video card initialization. The firmware interfaces are described under "Declaration ROM Operation," later in this chapter.

The FBC uses the parameters stored in the control registers to generate and control video data and timing signal output. The various gated inputs on the FBC are used to execute RAM read/write and refresh operations. RAM operations are more fully explained under "Video RAM," later in this chapter.

The control registers used by the FBC are mapped into Macintosh II main memory in the slot space assigned to the video card. The control address space is independent of the frame buffer data space. The following paragraphs briefly describe each of the parameters stored in the control registers.

Important

Your applications should never access the hardware directly because the locations and functions of the registers may change (and also because the registers won't be compatible with other manufacturers' cards). To maintain product compatibility across a possible variety of Macintosh video cards, and to allow for any future changes to the hardware, you are *strongly advised* to always use software interfaces (OS and Toolbox routines) to access the card whenever possible.

Base parameter

Base defines the offset from the base of the frame buffer RAM to the upper leftmost pixel in the display.

Length parameter

Length defines the screen width. It is equal to rowbytes/4, where rowbytes is the number of bytes between successively scanned lines. For an 8-bit per pixel, non-interlaced, 640-pixel wide screen, Length would be set to 160. For an interlaced display, Length would be set to 320, because interlaced displays scan every other line.

Rfsh parameter

Rfsh defines the number of screen rows in RAM refreshed per scan-line period.

Interlace parameter

Interlace sets the Frame Buffer Controller interlace mode. If Interlace is set to 1, the FBC operates in interlaced mode; otherwise, the FBC operates in non-interlaced mode.

Genlock parameter

Genlock sets the horizontal and vertical synchronization modes. When Genlock is set to 1, the synchronization signals are externally generated. This bit is normally set to 0, as many of the parameter definitions change when the FBC is in external synchronization mode.

Setup parameter

Setup defines the time required to synchronize the FBC pixel generation arrays with the FBC RAM timing arrays.

Polarity parameter

Polarity defines the sense of the system address bus at the FBC inputs. Polarity is set to 1 for Macintosh II, as the NuBus uses inverted sense (active low). Polarity is automatically set to 0 when /RESET is active. The declaration ROM sets Polarity to 1 after a reset.

Depth parameter

Depth defines the screen resolution in bits per pixel. The value of this parameter causes the FBC to prescale the pixel clock and multiplex the pixel data to produce the desired screen resolution. Depth must be set before /RESET is set to 1 so that the pixel clock generation circuitry has time to stabilize.

Reset parameter

Reset defines the state of the FBC. If Reset is set to 1, the FBC is in the normal state and all registers are considered to be valid. If Reset is equal to 0, the FBC is in the reset state, and all parameters except Reset are considered to be in an undefined state. Reset is the last parameter set by the declaration ROM during the intialization procedure.

Hsyncstart parameter

Hsyncstart is one of the six parameters that define the timing characteristics for a single scan line. Figure 11-2 diagrams a scan line by the regions used to define it. Refer to Figure 11-2 for all of the horizontal timing parameters.

Hsyncstart defines the length of the horizontal front porch. In Figure 11-2, Hsyncstart is equal to the duration, in **scaled pixel clock periods,** of region 5 minus 2 pixel clock periods.

The horizontal front porch is the duration of the signal that precedes the horizontal synchronization pulse.

A pixel clock period is the period of the pixel clock (PXCLK) signal. PXCLK is time scaled according to the screen resolution selected. Thus, a measurement in *scaled* pixel clock periods means the number of PXCLK periods *at the current resolution.*

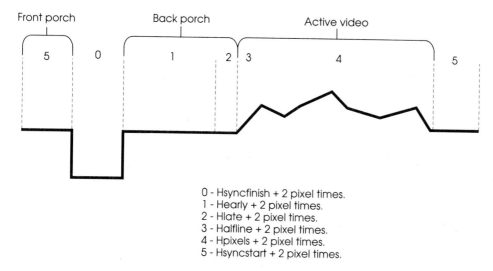

0 - Hsyncfinish + 2 pixel times.
1 - Hearly + 2 pixel times.
2 - Hlate + 2 pixel times.
3 - Halfline + 2 pixel times.
4 - Hpixels + 2 pixel times.
5 - Hsyncstart + 2 pixel times.

Figure 11-2
Scan line horizontal timing regions

Hsyncfinish parameter

Hsyncfinish is equal to the duration, in scaled pixel clock periods, of region 0 minus 2 scaled pixel clock periods.

The composite synchronization signal contains equalization pulses in accordance with EIA specification RS-170. The duration of these pulses is equal to Hsyncfinish divided by 2 scaled pixel clock periods.

Hearly parameter

Hearly is equal to the duration, in scaled pixel clock periods, of region 1 minus 2 scaled pixel clock periods.

The horizontal back porch is the duration of the signal that follows the horizontal synchronization pulse and precedes the active video region. The horizontal back porch is broken up into region 1 (Hearly) and region 2 (Hlate).

Hlate parameter

Hlate is equal to the duration, in scaled pixel clock periods, of region 2 minus 2 scaled pixel clock periods. The duration of region 2 is calculated by adding 3 processor clock periods to the worst-case time to finish a bus cycle. Hlate and Hearly combine to give the length of the horizontal back porch.

Halfline parameter

Halfline is equal to the duration, in scaled pixel clock periods, of region 3 minus 2 scaled pixel clock periods.

The end of region 3 marks the middle of the scan line and determines the point at which the RS-170 equalization pulses start.

Hpixels parameter

Hpixels is the number of pixels displayed in the active video region. The active video region is the interval between the middle of the scan line (the end of region 3) and the start of the horizontal front porch (the beginning of region 5). Hpixels is equal to the duration, in scaled pixel clock periods, of region 4 minus 2 scaled pixel clock periods.

Syncinterval parameter

The RS-170 composite synchronization signal contains vertical serrations. Syncinterval defines the duration of the interval between these vertical serrations. Syncinterval has no direct bearing on the length of the scan line.

Vfrontporch parameter

Vfrontporch is one of the four parameters that define the timing characteristics for *vertical* synchronization. Figure 11-3 diagrams a scan line by the vertical synchronization timing regions used to define it. Refer to Figure 11-3 for all of the vertical synchronization timing parameters.

Vfrontporch defines the length of the vertical front porch. In Figure 11-3, Vfrontporch is equal to the duration, in half scan line periods, of region 0 minus one half scan line period. The vertical front porch is the duration of the signal that precedes the vertical synchronization pulse. A half scan line period is a time period equal to one half the time required to write a scan line.

The RS-170 equalization pulses are inserted during the last three lines of Vfrontporch and the first three lines of Vbackporch.

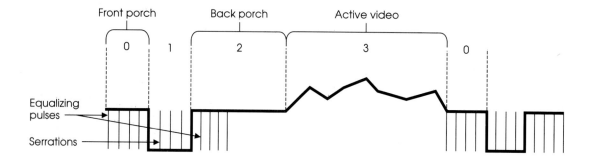

0 - Vfrontporch + 1 half line time.
1 - Vsyncfinish + 1 half line time.
2 - Vbackporch + 8 half line times.
3 - Vlines + 1 half line time.

Figure 11-3
Scan line vertical timing regions

Vsyncfinish parameter

Vsyncfinish defines the length of the vertical synchronization pulse period. In Figure 11-3, Vsyncfinish is equal to the duration, in half scan line periods, of region 1 minus one half scan line period. The RS-170 vertical serrations are inserted during Vsyncfinish. One serration is inserted for each half scan line period.

Vbackporch parameter

Vbackporch defines the length of the vertical back porch. The vertical back porch is the duration of the signal that follows the vertical synchronization pulse and precedes the active video signal. In Figure 11-3, Vbackporch is equal to the duration, in half scan line periods, of region 2 minus eight half scan line periods.

Vlines parameter

Vlines defines the length of the active video period. In Figure 11-3, Vlines is equal to the duration, in half scan line periods, of region 3 minus one half scan line period. For interlaced displays, Vlines is set to half the number of lines displayed during the active video period.

Video RAM

The video RAM consists of eight or sixteen 64 Kbit x 4, 150 nanosecond ICs for a memory configuration of 256 Kbytes or 512 Kbytes. The RAM ICs have a built-in shift register and separate serial port for video data, allowing more than 95 percent of the video RAM bandwidth to be available to the processor.

Of primary interest to you as a developer of a card or driver are NuBus operations to and from video RAM. Bus operations to RAM (transactions) are of two types:

☐ video RAM space writes and reads

☐ control space writes and reads

Figure 11-4 shows a timing diagram for a processor access to video RAM space, for writing and then reading. The typical sequence of functions is annotated on the figure; also shown are the start and acknowledge cycles that characterize a transaction as described in Chapters 2, "NuBus Overview," and 3, "NuBus Data Transfer."

❖ *Note:* The video card clock (20M) is twice the frequency of the NuBus clock (/CLK).

Key elements of the sequence are as follows:

1. The current bus master drives /START to asserted (low), places desired video RAM space *address* on the /AD31–/AD2 bus, and drives </TM1–/TM0,/AD1–/AD0> with the transfer mode. /TM1 is low when the first transaction in Figure 11-4 starts, indicating that a write transaction is underway.

2. Write output enable (/WROE) is asserted (low).

3. The video card decodes /ID3–/ID0 to determine whether it is in the slot currently being accessed by the current bus master; if so, then the card's /SLOT SELECT is asserted.

4. On the next rising (sampling) edge of the video clock (20M) RAM select (/RAMSEL) is asserted; this indicates that a RAM access is to be initiated on the next driving edge of the NuBus clock.

5. The RAM timing chain is commenced, driven by a state machine going sequentially through states 3, 2, 0, 1, and repeating; this machine controls a wait for the data from the bus master/processor to become ready, initiates row and column address strobes, and generates the RAM accesses to do the writing.

6. The bus master drives the /AD31–/AD0 lines with the *data* to be written and releases the /TM1–/TM0 lines and the /ACK line.

7. The video card drives the transaction response status onto the /TM1–/TM0 lines and asserts acknowledge (/ACK), notifying the bus master that the write transaction is completed.

8. The bus master releases the /AD31–/AD0 lines and drives the /ACK line to a determinate state.

9. The video card releases the /TM1–/TM0 lines and also releases acknowledge (/ACK), completing the write transaction.

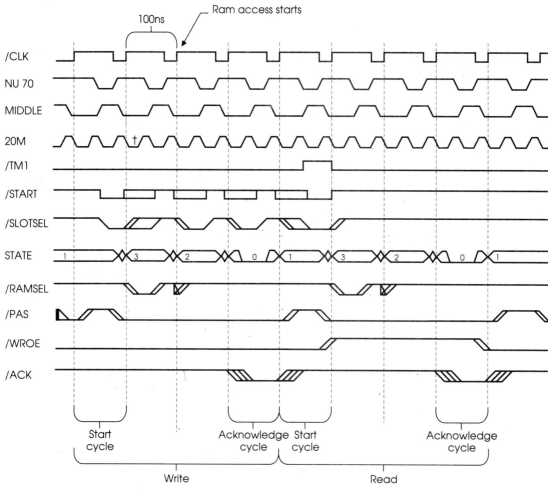

Figure 11-4
Access to RAM space

Color look-up table (CLUT)

The CLUT is the electrical interface between the FBC and the analog video output device. Digital video data is passed to the CLUT through the FBC. The CLUT converts the digital data representing index values to color values by table look up in RAM, then uses its 8-bit DACs to generate analog color signals. The CLUT provides RS-343A-compatible RGB video signals to the I/O connector at the rear of the video card.

The CLUT is a triple 8-bit RAMDAC. A RAMDAC has three channels (for red, green, and blue) of RAM and DAC integrated into one IC. It supports up to 256 simultaneous colors from a 16.8 million color palette.

The RAM within the CLUT is initialized by Color QuickDraw with default color transformation values using the video driver loaded from the declaration ROM. Color QuickDraw also provides utilities, via the video driver, to read and modify the color palette.

Figure 11-5 shows the timing for a processor access to control space in RAM for the purpose of writing to the color look-up table.

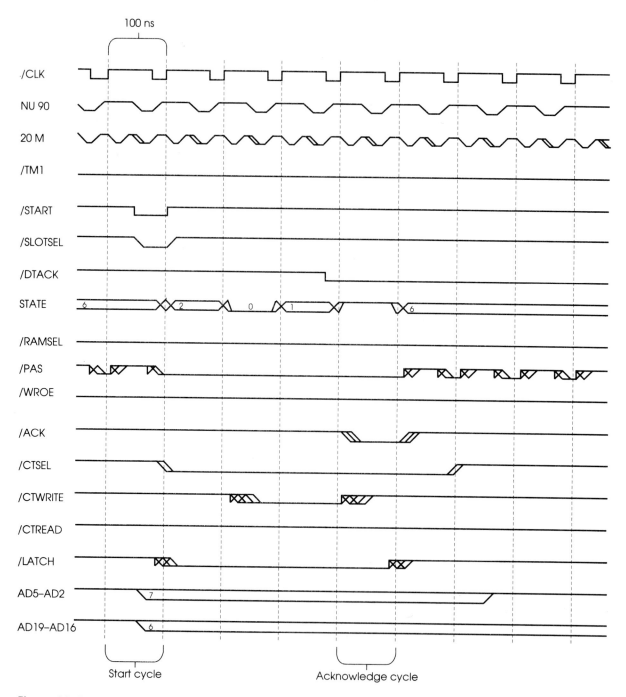

Figure 11-5
Access to control space for CLUT write

Horizontal and vertical scan timing

Figure 11-6 relates the blanking, synchronizing, and active video regions of the video scan waveforms to the dot or pixel time. H is the time for one horizontal line, including retrace. A dot is the time required to draw a single pixel.

Horizontal timing

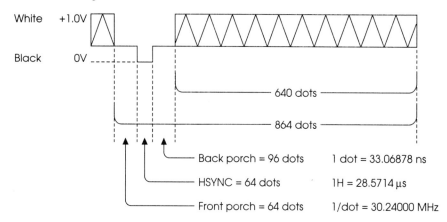

White +1.0V

Black 0V

640 dots

864 dots

Back porch = 96 dots   1 dot = 33.06878 ns

HSYNC = 64 dots   1H = 28.5714 µs

Front porch = 64 dots   1/dot = 30.24000 MHz

Vertical timing

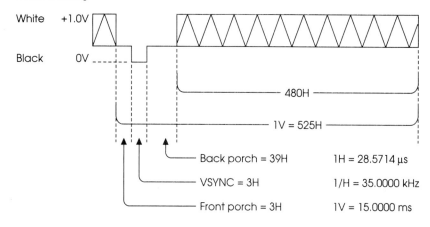

White +1.0V

Black 0V

480H

1V = 525H

Back porch = 39H   1H = 28.5714 µs

VSYNC = 3H   1/H = 35.0000 kHz

Front porch = 3H   1V = 15.0000 ms

Vsync detail

Csync detail

Note: Voltage levels to comply with EIA specification RS–343–A,
except Csync, which is a TTL signal.

Figure 11-6
Horizontal and vertical scan timing

Declaration ROM operation

The declaration ROM contains all information required to identify and utilize the capabilities of the peripheral card it is installed on. In the case of the Macintosh II Video Card, the declaration ROM identifies the card as a video device manufactured by Apple and identifies the particular model. The declaration ROM also provides a list of predefined video modes, each element of which specifies all the parameters of the display unique to that mode, including horizontal and vertical size, pixel size, rowbytes of a scan line, and the number of video pages available at this screen resolution.

As described in the earlier sections of this chapter, the video card is highly programmable, and as a result, the number of possible video modes is enormous. A useful subset, optimized for the Apple displays, have been selected, and are included in the declaration ROM. The list characterizing each video mode also specifies a software driver, specific to the card hardware and located in the ROM, that is loaded into CPU memory by the Slot Manager at startup time. This driver is equivalent to the firmware on traditional peripheral cards; object code is not normally executed over the bus.

The declaration ROM also includes special code, called the PrimaryInit, that performs key, one-time initialization to the card hardware when executed.

These three elements

☐ the configuration data

☐ the driver

☐ and the primary initialization code

together allow the video card to be installed into a system, recognized, and used without having to run any special configuration programs, or without adding any code to the system file of the host system.

Usually, it is not necessary to access the slot information or the driver directly from the application; see Figure 11-7. Color QuickDraw and the Color Manager in the Macintosh II ROM manage all transactions to the card and its driver. For example, the InitGDevice routine in Color QuickDraw (documented in the graphics devices chapter of *Inside Macintosh,* Volume V) issues all the appropriate calls to change the video mode, load the CLUT, and perform other hardware maintenance tasks, as well as updating system variables pertinent to the affected video device. Selection of a video mode is made possible by system software such as Monitors and a Control Panel module that graphically presents all possible modes for a video device (as enumerated in the declaration ROM) and allows interactive selection. By using system code such as QuickDraw and the Control Panel, application writing can be simplified as well as present a more uniform interface to the user.

The declaration ROM of the Macintosh II Video Card has some unique features. Because the card is available in two configurations—256K and 512K RAM—a number of mode conflicts arise. Most notably, the 256K version of the card does not support 8-bit mode, and each common mode has a different number of video pages available on the two cards. To resolve this problem, the card includes two complete slot resource lists; one for the 256K card and another for the fully stocked card.

At startup time, both slot resource lists are installed into the system's slot resource table. When the primary initialization code of the video card is executed, in addition to initializing the FBC, it performs a size test on the amount of available video RAM, and removes the slot resource list that does not apply. The 256K version of the slot resource list includes configuration information only for 1-, 2-, and 4-bit video modes as well as the appropriate number of video pages available. Normally the video mode of a card in a Macintosh II system is set using a Control Panel module called *Monitors*. (See the chapter on the Control Panel in *Inside Macintosh*, Volume V, for more information on Control Panel modules.) Monitors finds the available video modes of a video card by examining the declaration ROM's information. By implementing the declaration ROM in the manner described here, a single declaration ROM serves both configurations of the video card without Monitors having to verify device-dependent information (such as memory size).

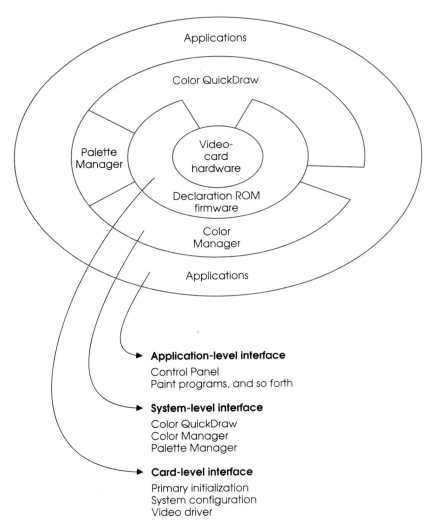

Figure 11-7
Firmware levels

Chapter 9, "NuBus Driver Design," contains a listing of code for a possible video card driver. A driver like this might be part of the declaration ROM code for a video card.

Card connectors

The Macintosh II Video Card contains two connectors. The appearance of the card and the location of the connectors are as shown in Foldout 1 at the back of the book. The connection to the NuBus is through the 96-pin Euro-DIN connector shown in Chapter 7, Figure 7-1. The pinout of this connector is given in Table 6-3.

The small DB-15 connector at the rear of the card provides the red, blue, and green video output signals and the synch signal. The pinout of the DB-15 is in Table 11-1.

Table 11-1
Output connector
pin assignments

Pin	Signal
1	GND
2	RED
3	/CSYNCH
4	GND
5	GREEN
6	GND
7	No connection
8	No connection
9	BLUE
10	No connection
11	GND
12	No connection
13	GND
14	GND
15	No connection

Part II

The Macintosh SE Interface

Introduction

About Part II

The Macintosh SE-Bus is the subject of Part II of this book.

Chapter 12 provides a block diagram of the complete Macintosh SE main logic board and an overview of computer operation. The chapter then describes the SE-Bus features. Throughout Part II a word means a 16-bit word.

Chapter 13 contains the electrical information you need:

☐ the expansion connector pinout and signal description

☐ expansion card load limits and drive requirements

☐ how to access the Macintosh SE electronics

☐ a map of available address space

☐ guidelines to minimize electromagnetic interference

☐ power budget for each supply voltage

Chapter 14 details the physical information you need:

☐ mechanical drawings of the main logic board and the expansion connector

☐ design guide for an expansion card showing the mating connector, envelope of space available, and mechanical support provisions

☐ a source of a blank prototyping card, with connector

☐ guidelines for heat dissipation

☐ considerations involved with product safety

Chapter 15 provides design guidance for connecting your expansion card to an external peripheral device through the accessory access port. Mechanical drawings and EMI guidelines are included.

Chapter 16 describes a proven design of a simple disk controller card that uses the SE-Bus very successfully.

Chapter 12

The Macintosh SE Architecture

This chapter provides an overview of the structure and organization of the Macintosh SE computer. It places the internal expansion bus and connector in context within the total computing machine. Subsequent chapters provide the information needed to design expansion cards compatible with the SE-Bus and the expansion connector. This chapter assumes you're familiar with the basic operation of microprocessor-based devices.

Overview of the hardware

Features of the Macintosh SE are

☐ 800K internal floppy disk drive

☐ optional internal disk or an optional second 800K internal floppy disk drive

☐ 8 MHz MC68000 processor

☐ gate array implementation on the main logic board of previously used PAL and discrete logic devices

☐ 256K ROM

☐ 1MB RAM, expandable to 2MB, 2.5MB, or 4MB

☐ two mini-8 connectors for serial ports, compatible with those on the Macintosh Plus

☐ synchronous modem support on one serial port

☐ Apple Desktop Bus™ (ADB) mouse and ADB keyboard with built-in cursor keys and numeric keypad

☐ SCSI high-speed peripheral port

☐ external connectors: two serial ports, two Apple Desktop Bus connectors, a SCSI connector, a floppy disk drive connector, and an audio jack

☐ long-life lithium battery for clock and calendar

☐ provision for an internal custom expansion card to communicate with the SE-Bus

☐ new swing-away mounting to allow insertion of logic board with optional expansion card present

Hardware architecture

A block diagram of the Macintosh SE computer is shown in Figure 12-1. The following discussion is brief and intended primarily to show the place of the SE-Bus and internal expansion connector in the machine architecture. For a complete description of hardware operation, see the *Macintosh Family Hardware Reference* manual. A higher level overview is available in the *Technical Introduction to the Macintosh Family*.

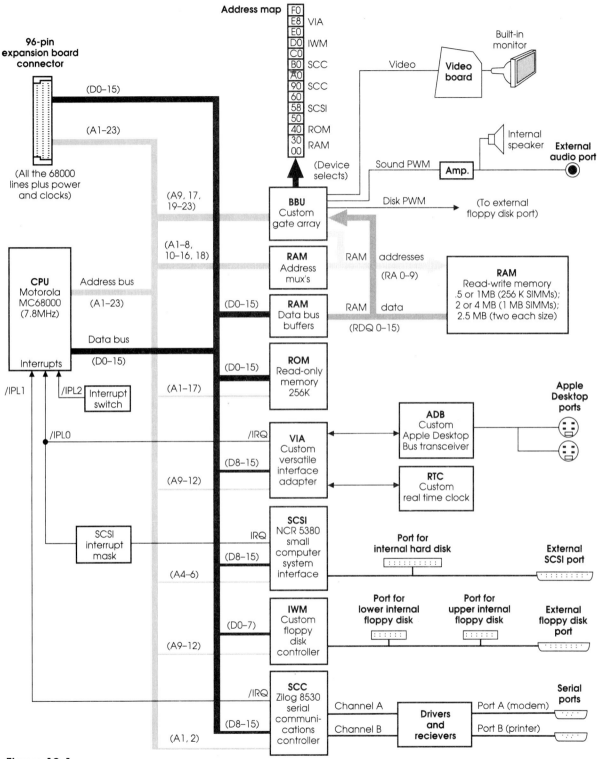

Figure 12-1
Block diagram of the Macintosh SE

The Macintosh SE contains the Motorola MC68000 microprocessor operating at 7.8336 megahertz, random access memory (RAM), read-only memory (ROM), and five I/O chips that enable the microprocessor to communicate with external devices. These I/O chips are

☐ an Apple custom Versatile Interface Adapter (VIA) for communicating with the ADB transceiver which, in turn, communicates with the mouse, keyboard, and other devices on the Apple Desktop Bus (the VIA also communicates with the real time clock—RTC)

❖ *Note:* The VIA performs several other functions such as selecting between the two video buffers, selecting between the two internal floppy disk drives (if present), selecting synchronous modem timing on serial port A, receiving vertical sweep blanking interrupts, turning sound on or off, and so forth.

☐ an NCR 5380 SCSI (small computer system interface) for high speed data transfer with the optional internal hard disk or other SCSI devices through the external SCSI port

☐ a Zilog Z8530 Serial Communications Controller (SCC) for asynchronous serial communication (also synchronous modem support)

☐ an Apple custom chip, called the IWM (Integrated Woz Machine), for control of floppy disk drives

☐ an Apple custom chip, called the BBU (Bob Bailey Unit), for video and sound control and for generating device-select signals

The Macintosh SE uses memory-mapped I/O, which means that each device in the system is accessed by reading or writing to specific locations in the address space of the computer. The BBU contains logic that selects the device being accessed, and that device then responds in the appropriate manner.

The MC68000 can directly access 16 megabytes of address space. In the Macintosh SE, this address space is divided into four equal sections. The first four megabytes are for RAM, the second four are for ROM and SCSI, the third are for the SCC, and the last four are for the IWM and the VIA. Because the 24-bit addresses are incompletely decoded, the locations or registers appear at many addresses (aliases) within the block of memory assigned to that device. This means that the contents of a location or register may be accessed through any of these many aliases.

RAM

RAM is the working memory of the system.

When the Macintosh SE is first turned on, RAM appears at $60 0000. (For a system with more than 2MB of RAM, only the top *row* of RAM appears.) ROM is at $00 0000 (in addition to its normal location at $40 0000), and the 256 bytes of exception vectors are in ROM. Following the first normal ROM access or SCSI access ($40 0000 through $5F FFFF), RAM appears at $00 0000 and ROM appears only at $40 0000.

The first 256 bytes of RAM (addresses $00 0000 through $00 00FF) are used by the MC68000 as exception vectors; these are the addresses of the routines that gain control whenever an exception such as an interrupt or a trap occurs. RAM also contains the system and application **heaps,** the **stack,** and other information used by applications. For a complete map of the address ranges used in the Macintosh SE, see Figure 13-4 in the next chapter. In addition, the following hardware devices share the use of RAM with the MC68000:

□ the video display, which reads the information for the display from one of two screen buffers

□ the sound generator, which reads its information from a sound buffer

□ the disk speed controller (used only with an external, single-sided floppy disk drive), which shares its data space with the sound buffer

On the Macintosh 512 and Macintosh Plus, the MC68000 accesses to RAM are interleaved (alternated) with the video display's accesses during the active portion of a screen scan line. On the Macintosh SE, the MC68000 is given three accesses to every one for video, and each video access takes two words, compared to one in the Macintosh 512 or Macintosh Plus. The sound generator and disk speed controller are given the first access before each scan line. At all other times, the MC68000 has uninterrupted access to RAM.

❖ *Note:* The following information is useful in designing program timing loops. For a Macintosh 512 or a Macintosh Plus, the RAM access rate is 1.96 megabytes/second (MB/sec) during a horizontal scan line and 3.92 MB/sec during horizontal and vertical blanking intervals, producing an average access rate of 2.56 MB/sec. For a Macintosh SE, the corresponding numbers are 2.94 MB/sec during a scan line and 3.92 MB/sec during blanking, for an average of 3.22 MB/sec.

ROM

ROM is the system's permanent read-only memory.

When the Macintosh SE is first turned on, a second image of ROM appears at
$00 0000, so that ROM can supply the MC68000 with the exception vectors ($00 0000
through $00 00FF). Following the first access to the address range $40 0000 through
$5F FFFF (ROM or SCSI), the image of ROM at $00 0000 is replaced by RAM.

The base address, $40 0000, is available as the constant romStart and is also stored in
the global variable ROMBase. ROM contains the routines for the Toolbox and
Operating System, and the various system traps. Because the ROM is used exclusively
by the MC68000, it's always accessed at the maximum rate of 3.92 MB/sec.

Device I/O

The address space reserved for the device I/O contains blocks devoted to each of the
devices within the computer. This region begins at address $50 0000 and continues to
the highest address at $FF FFFF.

The SE-Bus expansion interface

The Macintosh SE is the first member of the Macintosh family that has the capacity
for internal hardware expansion. Many developers and users have shown an
increasing interest in adding their own hardware inside the Macintosh, and in
accessing internal hardware signals from outside of the Macintosh. The
Macintosh SE expansion bus has been designed to help these designers add reliable
and elegant custom hardware to the Macintosh.

The SE-Bus

The primary feature of the Macintosh SE expansion bus is a 96-pin Euro-DIN
connector providing unbuffered access to all of the Macintosh MC68000 signals. This
includes the complete microprocessor address bus, data bus, and control bus. In
addition, extensive power and grounding are provided, as well as critical high-speed
timing signals. The SE-Bus supports high-speed **DMA** into the Macintosh RAM,
allows coprocessors to share the Macintosh address and data bus, and allocates
generous portions of the address space for new peripherals.

Additional support for expansion

A higher-capacity power supply (than in the Macintosh Plus) and a fan ensure that power and cooling can easily accomodate additional custom electronics. The Macintosh SE supports one internal expansion card of approximately four inches by eight inches in area.

A 96-pin connector provides one mounting point for an expansion card, and there are holes at the opposite side of the Macintosh logic board for two mounting posts. See Figure 14-2 for a drawing of these mounting provisions. The Macintosh SE logic board and chassis have been designed to allow mounting and removal of the logic board while it is joined to an expansion card.

Several new features allow a designer to route cables from an expansion card up to a bracket and access door at the rear of the case. The bracket can hold custom connectors on a small connector board that may also contain filter-electronics. Chapter 15 contains drawings of the means for connecting from an expansion card to external devices through the accessory access port.

Third-party products that adhere to the recommended expansion guidelines discussed in Chapters 13 through 16, use the Apple-supplied expansion features, and do not require physical alteration of the Macintosh SE will not void the Apple Limited Warranty.

The MC68000 microprocessor and its bus have been extensively documented by Motorola, Inc. Please refer to their document number AD1814R5, dated March 1985, and titled *MC68000 16/32-Bit Microprocessor* for design assistance with the expansion card to MC68000 interface. Developers of custom expansion cards, following the guidelines in Chapters 13 through 16, may choose to offer cards such as the following:

□ custom video card

□ network communication interface card

□ modem card

□ coprocessor or accelerator card

The foregoing list is not intended to limit or authorize, in any way, the types of expansion cards that may be developed.

In summary, then, custom card expansion of the Macintosh SE is supported by these features:

□ Euro-DIN type 96-pin expansion connector that provides power, timing, and direct access to the SE-Bus and to the MC68000

□ standoff mounting for card physical support

□ high capacity power supply and cooling fan

□ main logic board layout and installation features improved from earlier Macintosh models

□ accessory access port provided at housing rear, for custom external connector

Chapter 13

Electrical Design Guide for Macintosh SE Cards

This chapter provides an electrical design guide for your custom expansion card. Most cards will have a connector that mates with the 96-pin connector on the Macintosh SE main logic board. The chapter covers the following topics:

☐ electrical description of the expansion connector

☐ signal mnemonics and descriptions

☐ accessing the Macintosh SE electronics from an expansion card

☐ available address space

☐ electromagnetic interference (EMI) guidelines for expansion cards

Electrical description of the expansion connector

Figure 13-1 gives the pin-out for the 96-pin expansion connector (socket) on the Macintosh SE logic board, as seen from above.

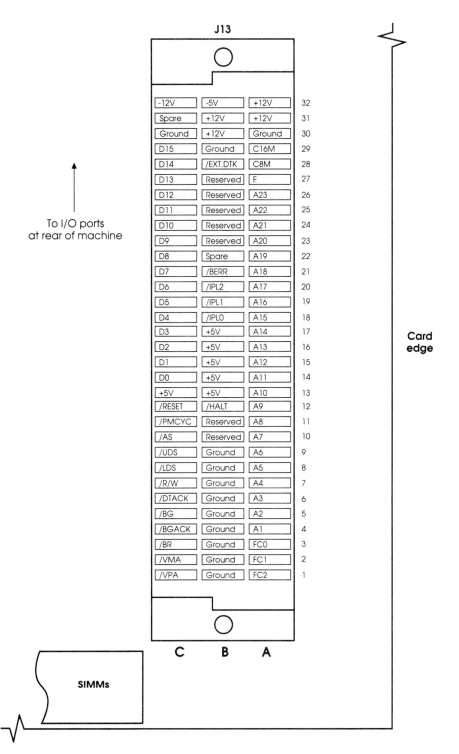

J13

C	B	A	
-12V	-5V	+12V	32
Spare	+12V	+12V	31
Ground	+12V	Ground	30
D15	Ground	C16M	29
D14	/EXT.DTK	C8M	28
D13	Reserved	E	27
D12	Reserved	A23	26
D11	Reserved	A22	25
D10	Reserved	A21	24
D9	Reserved	A20	23
D8	Spare	A19	22
D7	/BERR	A18	21
D6	/IPL2	A17	20
D5	/IPL1	A16	19
D4	/IPL0	A15	18
D3	+5V	A14	17
D2	+5V	A13	16
D1	+5V	A12	15
D0	+5V	A11	14
+5V	+5V	A10	13
/RESET	/HALT	A9	12
/PMCYC	Reserved	A8	11
/AS	Reserved	A7	10
/UDS	Ground	A6	9
/LDS	Ground	A5	8
/R/W	Ground	A4	7
/DTACK	Ground	A3	6
/BG	Ground	A2	5
/BGACK	Ground	A1	4
/BR	Ground	FC0	3
/VMA	Ground	FC1	2
/VPA	Ground	FC2	1

To I/O ports
at rear of machine

Card
edge

SIMMs

Figure 13-1
Expansion connector pinout

Table 13-1 gives signal descriptions and the load presented, or drive available, to each pin on an expansion card inserted into the 96-pin expansion connector.

An example may be helpful in interpreting the column headed *Loading or drive capability*. The /RESET line is shown as presenting a load of 300µA/6mA, 50pF. This is the maximum expected load that an expansion card must drive when sending a /RESET signal to the Macintosh SE logic board. The DC load is given in the *signal high/signal low* format. This means that the expansion card driver must drive a load of up to 300µA when it drives /RESET high (logic 1), and a load of up to 6mA when it drives /RESET low (logic 0). The AC load is given as 50pF, the maximum capacitance to ground presented by the Macintosh SE logic board to AC signals (or signal transitions) from the expansion card. The notation "Open collector; 1K ohm pullup" in the table means that the /RESET line is normally driven open collector: it is *only* driven low, and a 1K ohm pullup resistor on the Macintosh SE logic board returns the line to a logic 1.

Correspondingly, /RESET presents a drive of 40µA/.4mA, 30pF. This is the maximum amount of drive from the Macintosh SE logic board that is available to receiving integrated circuits on an expansion card. The /RESET line of the Macintosh SE can drive an expansion card DC load of up to 40 µA in the high (logic 1) state, or up to .4mA in the low (logic 0) state. The AC drive is given as 30pF, the maximum capacitance to ground that an expansion card may present to AC signals (or signal transitions) from the Macintosh SE /RESET line.

The C8M and C16M clock outputs are specified to drive one 74LS input (a standard 74LS input load is 20µA high, .2mA low) and 20pF. All other outputs have been specified to drive two 74LS inputs, and 30pF.

In most cases, these drive limitations are imposed to protect the noise and timing margins of the Macintosh SE logic board. Expansion cards requiring more drive, or more than about two inches of trace length, should buffer these signals before distributing them to the effective loads on the card or to external devices connected through the Accessory Access Port.

Where "load:" is in parentheses, the pin carries a signal that is usually an output driven by the MC68000, but that is tri-stated by the MC68000 after responding to a bus request. When tri-stated by the MC68000, this pin may be driven by an expansion card.

Table 13-1
Expansion connector signals, loading or driving capability

Connector		Signal	Signal	Input or	Loading or driving
Row	Pin	name	description	output	capability (high/low)
A	1	FC2	Function code 2	Output (Input)	Drive: 40µA/.4mA, 30pF (Load: 100µA/100µA, 50pF)
A	2	FC1	Function code 1	Output (Input)	Drive: 40µA/.4mA, 30pF (Load: 100µA/100µA, 50pF)
A	3	FC0	Function code 0	Output (Input)	Drive: 40µA/.4mA, 30pF (Load: 100µA/100µA, 50pF)
A	4–26	A1–23	Address 1–23	In/Out	Load: 250µA/1mA, 100pF Drive: 40µA/.4mA, 30pF
A	27	E	E (enable) clock	Output	Drive: 40µA/.4mA, 30pF
A	28	C8M	7.8336 MHz MC68000 clock	Output	Drive: 20µA/.2mA, 20pF
A	29	C16M	15.6672 MHz gate array and IWM clock	Output	Drive: 20µA/.2mA, 20pF
A	30	GND	Logic ground		
A	31	+12V	+12 volts	Output	Drive: 150mA total, from all +12V pins
A	32	+12V	+12 volts	Output	(see the section "Power Budget")
B	1–9	GND	Logic ground		
B	10	Reserved	For future Apple use; do not connect		
B	11	Reserved	For future Apple use; do not connect		
B	12	/HALT	MC68000 Halt	In/Out	Load: 300µA/6mA, 50pF Drive: 0µA/0µA (Connected to /RESET, pin C-12)
B	13–17	+5V	+5 volts	Output	Drive: 1.5 A total, from all +5V pins (see the section "Power Budget")
B	18	/IPL0	Interrupt level 0 (VIA, SCSI.IRQ)	In/Out	Load: 100µA/2mA, 50pF Drive: 40µA/.4mA, 30pF (Open collector; 3.3K ohm pullup)

(continued)

Table 13-1 (continued)
Expansion connector signals, loading or driving capability

Connector		Signal	Signal	Input or	Loading or driving
Row	Pin	name	description	output	capability (high/low)
B	19	/IPL1	Interrupt level 1 (SCC)	In/Out	Load: 100μA/2mA, 50pF Drive: 40μA/.4mA, 30pF (Open collector; 3.3K ohm pullup)
B	20	/IPL2	Interrupt level 2 (NMI switch)	In/Out	Load: 100μA/2mA, 50pF Drive: 40μA/.4mA, 30pF (Open collector; 3.3K ohm pullup)
B	21	/BERR	Bus error	In/Out	Load: 100μA/2mA, 50pF Drive: 40μA/.4mA, 30pF (Open collector; 3.3K ohm pullup)
B	22	Spare	Not connected		
B	23–27	Reserved	For future Apple use; do not connect		
B	28	/EXT.DTK	External /DTACK (tri-states main board's /DTACK)	Input	Load: 100μA/2mA, 50pF (3.3K ohm pullup)
B	29	GND	Logic ground		
B	30	+12V	+12 volts	Output	Drive: 150mA total, from all +12V pins
B	31	+12V	+12 volts	Output	(see the section "Power Budget")
B	32	–5V	–5 volts	Output	Drive: 100mA
C	1	/VPA	Valid periph. address	Output	Drive: 40μA/.4mA, 30pF
C	2	/VMA	Valid memory address	Output (Input)	Drive: 40μA/.4mA, 30pF (Load: 100μA/100μA, 50pF)
C	3	/BR	Bus request	Input	Load: 100μA/2mA, 50pF (3.3K ohm pullup)
C	4	/BGACK	Bus grant acknowledge	Input	Load: 100μA/2mA, 50pF (3.3K ohm pullup)
C	5	/BG	Bus grant	Output	Drive: 40μA/.4mA, 30pF
C	6	/DTACK	Data transfer acknowledge	In/Out	Load: 100μA/2mA, 50pF Drive: 40μA/.4mA, 30pF (3.3K ohm pullup, /EXT.DTK low, tri-states main board's /DTACK)

Connector		Signal	Signal	Input or	Loading or driving
Row	Pin	name	description	output	capability (high/low)
C	7	R/W	Read/write	Output (Input)	Drive: 40µA/.4mA, 30pF (Load: 200µA/2mA, 50pF)
C	8	/LDS	Lower data strobe	Output (Input)	Drive: 40µA/.4mA, 30pF (Load: 100µA/1mA, 50pF)
C	9	/UDS	Upper data strobe	Output (Input)	Drive: 40µA/.4mA, 30pF (Load: 100µA/1mA, 50pF)
C	10	/AS	Address strobe	Output (Input)	Drive: 40µA/.4mA, 30pF (Load: 200µA/3.2mA, 50pF; 3.3K ohm pullup)
C	11	/PMCYC	Processor memory cycle	Output	Drive: 40µA/.4mA, 30pF (High during video access to RAM)
C	12	/RESET	System reset	In/Out	Load: 300µA/6mA, 50pF Drive: 40µA/.4mA, 30pF (Open collector; 1K ohm pullup) (Connected to /HALT, pin B-12)
C	13	+5V	+5 volts	Output	Drive: 1.5A total, from all +5V pins (see the section "Power Budget")
C	14–29	D0–15	Data bus, bits 0–15	In/Out	Load: 250µA/1mA, 100pF Drive: 40µA/.4mA, 30pF
C	30	GND	Logic ground		
C	31	Spare	Not connected		
C	32	–12V	–12 volts	Output	Drive: 100mA

Functional description of the MC68000 signals

Table 13-2 lists the MC68000 signals available at the Macintosh SE expansion connector and describes their function.

Table 13-2
MC68000 signal descriptions

Mnemonic	Description
FC0–FC2	Function code lines.
A1–A23	Address lines.
E	E (enable) clock.
C8M	Microprocessor clock = 7.8336 MHz = C16M divided by 2.
C16M	Gate array clock = 15.6672 MHz.
/HALT	Halt. Wired directly to /RESET.
/IPL0–/IPL2	Interrupt priority level lines.
/BERR	Bus error. Generated by gate array due to SCSI access timeout. Actually /BERR is generated whenever /AS remains low for more than about 250 ms.)
/EXT.DTK	Pulled low to put the gate array's /DTACK output into a high-impedance state. The expansion card is then responsible for generating the /DTACK signal (as an output to the microprocessor, through the /DTACK signal line).
/VPA	Valid peripheral address. Supplied by the gate array, coincident with /AS, for any access to VPA space ($E0 0000 to $FF FFFF).
/VMA	Valid memory address.
/BR	Bus request.
/BGACK	Bus grant acknowledge.
/BG	Bus grant.

Table 13-2 (continued)
MC68000 signal descriptions

Mnemonic	Description
/DTACK	Data transfer acknowledge. In normal operation, /AS falls in S2 and the gate array supplies /DTACK in S4 of accesses to any address in the range $00 0000 to $DF FFFF. If /AS falls after S3, /DTACK is supplied in S0 of the next access cycle (except for RAM accesses, which wait until S4 of the next cycle). /DTACK may be held off to wait for DRQ (DMA request from SCSI) in pseudo-DMA-mode SCSI accesses, to separate two successive accesses to the SCC, or to wait for a RAM access by video. /DTACK is not supplied for accesses to /VPA address space ($E0 0000 to $FF FFFF).
	Gate array generation of /DTACK can be suppressed (put into a high-impedance state) by pulling the /EXT.DTK line low; this allows /DTACK to be externally generated by an expansion card.
R/W	Read/write.
/LDS	Lower data strobe.
/UDS	Upper data strobe
/AS	Address strobe.
/PMCYC	Processor memory cycle. Used to synchronize with the gate array for RAM accesses. /PMCYC is low when RAM is available for microprocessor accesses and is high during video accesses. /PMCYC is always high during S0. See timing diagram, Figure 13-2.
/RESET	Reset. Wired directly to /HALT.
D0-D15	Data bus.

Accessing the Macintosh SE electronics from an expansion card

An expansion card slave or peripheral I/O device simply occupies an available spot in the Macintosh SE address space (see Figure 13-4 later in the chapter), and the Macintosh SE can then access the card just as it accesses any of its own I/O devices.

The microprocessor on an expansion card (a coprocessor) has a more complex task than the microprocessor on the main logic board. Of course, the coprocessor can do its own work indefinitely, while the MC68000 of the Macintosh continues to function normally, provided the expansion card's electronics are sufficiently isolated from the Macintosh SE electronics. For meaningful results, however, most expansion card coprocessors will eventually need to access the I/O devices and RAM on the Macintosh SE logic board. To do this, the coprocessor requests the bus from the Macintosh SE MC68000 (using /BR), the MC68000 grants the request (using /BG) and tri-states itself off the bus at the end of that bus cycle; the coprocessor then takes over as bus master (using /BGACK). At this point, the expansion card's coprocessor has complete access to all of the Macintosh SE electronics.

Accessing I/O devices from an expansion card

For most of the Macintosh I/O devices, the timing of an access is managed entirely by the coprocessor. The coprocessor puts the device's address on the address bus and issues address strobe (/AS). For devices in the address range $00 0000 through $DF FFFF, the custom gate array (BBU, see Figure 12-1) responds by selecting the correct device and issuing /DTACK. If you, the card designer, need to supply a different /DTACK on that line, the gate array's /DTACK output can be put in tri-state by pulling the /EXT.DTK line low.

When a device is accessed in the range $E0 0000 through $FF FFFF (the VIA, for example), the BBU supplies /VPA instead of /DTACK. In normal operation, the MC68000 on the Macintosh SE logic board then responds to /VPA by providing the VIA chip select /VMA, timed correctly to the E clock. After removing itself from the bus by tri-state control, however, the MC68000 continues to generate its E clock but no longer provides /VMA. This means an expansion card coprocessor must correctly synchronize its VIA selection (using /VMA) and VIA accesses to the timing of the MC68000 E clock. The coprocessor can accept /VPA as its /DTACK, or provide its own.

Accessing RAM from an expansion card

When an expansion card coprocessor accesses the RAM on the Macintosh SE logic board, the timing of these accesses is much more tightly constrained, compared to accessing Macintosh I/O devices. Even if an expansion card coprocessor has its own on-card RAM, it will usually need to access the Macintosh SE RAM at least to update the information on the screen. This activity is always necessary because the information displayed on the Macintosh screen is always taken from the Macintosh RAM, regardless of any other RAM in the system.

As the designer of an expansion card, you may wish to synchronize the card's Macintosh RAM accesses (using /PMCYC) to avoid contention with the RAM accesses by Macintosh video circuitry. During the active portion of a screen scan line, the video uses one out of every four possible RAM accesses. These video accesses come at certain fixed times, regardless of any other activity in the system such as an expansion card coprocessor taking over the bus, or accesses to any I/O device or to the RAM itself. See Figure 13-2 for the timing of video versus processor accesses. If a coprocessor begins an access to Macintosh RAM during a video access, the coprocessor access is simply held off (/DTACK is not provided) until the following RAM-access time.

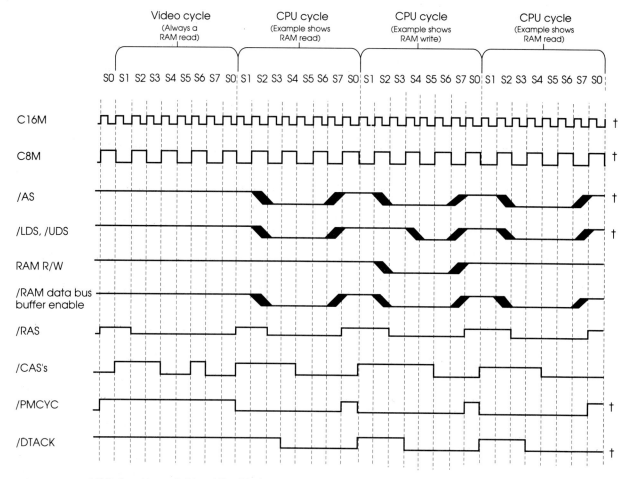

† This signal is available at the 96-pin expansion card connector.

Figure 13-2
Timing of video and MC68000 accesses to RAM

Furthermore, a coprocessor must synchronize its accesses to the state machine in the BBU. This gate array is designed to generate all of the RAM control signals at the correct times. The following information will help you synchronize an expansion card coprocessor to the RAM electronics on the Macintosh SE logic board.

The BBU operates with an internal state machine that generates 16 states (S0 to SF, numbered in hex), clocked by C16M. This state machine comes up randomly, and then counts through the 16 states continuously. The state counter is not affected by anything else in the system.

There are two types of basic RAM-access cycles: video/sound cycles and processor (CPU) cycles. Either type of RAM-access cycle occupies eight state-machine states. Video/sound cycles, when they occur, are always in states S8 to SF, while processor cycles can be either in states S0 to S7 or in states S8 to SF. To simplify discussion, however, the eight states of any RAM-access cycle are numbered S0 to S7. See Figure 13-2.

A video/sound cycle occurs as a result of specific counts of the video counter. A video cycle reads two words of data from the video buffer in RAM into the gate array's video shift register. A sound cycle is similar to a video cycle, except that a single word from the sound/disk-speed buffer in RAM is loaded into the gate array's sound and disk-speed counters.

A processor cycle, during which any processor (either on the main logic board or on an expansion card) may access RAM, can take place whenever a video/sound cycle is not occurring. If a processor initiates a RAM access during a video/sound cycle, the processor's RAM access is held off (/DTACK is not generated) until the video/sound cycle is complete. A processor can access devices other than RAM at any time, even during video/sound cycles.

The BBU requires that a processor must not begin RAM accesses at random times. In normal operation, it expects any processor to behave more or less like an MC68000, which asserts /AS in S2 (see Figure 13-3 for details). The MC68000 in the Macintosh SE is automatically synchronized to the state machine in the BBU by the processor's receipt of /DTACK, which the gate array always asserts in S4. An expansion card can synchronize itself to the state machine in the BBU by monitoring the signal /PMCYC. See Figure 13-2 for the operation of /PMCYC. /PMCYC always falls in S1 of an eight-state processor cycle. A falling-edge detector triggered by C16M can be used to find the falling edge of /PMCYC, and therefore S1.

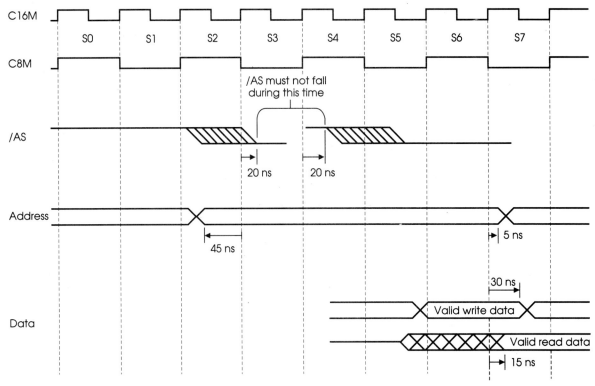

Figure 13-3
Timing for reading and writing RAM from an expansion card

Pertinent timing requirements, from Figure 13-3 are as follows:

□ minimum address setup time before /AS (address strobe) falls is 15 ns

□ minimum address setup time to start of S3 is 45 ns unless /AS falls after start of S3, in which case the minimum address setup time to /AS is 45 ns

□ address must remain valid through the first 5 ns of S7

□ /AS falling must occur not later than 20 ns into S3. If /AS has not fallen by that time, /AS must not fall until after the first 20 ns of S4 (data will be read or written in the next RAM access)

□ /DTACK rises 25 ns, maximum, following start of an odd S-state after /AS rises

□ write data to the RAM must be valid from the start of S6 through the first 30 ns of S7 (when /CAS falls)

□ read data from the RAM will be valid from 15 ns into S7 until /CAS rises at the end of S0, or until /AS rises, whichever occurs first

❖ *Note:* Clock C8M is shown only for its relation to the MC68000 state sequence. Actually, C8M is delayed relative to C16M by up to 30 ns.

Note to RAM access discussion

The coprocessor on an expansion card should operate very much like the MC68000 of the Macintosh SE when accessing the Macintosh SE RAM. In normal operation, therefore, an expansion card presents its addresses in S1, asserts /AS in S2, and receives /DTACK in S4. The following information is presented only for those designers who want to know, for some reason, exactly how far they may deviate from this normal method of operation.

To speed up RAM access, the Macintosh SE gate array internally generates a RAS-Enable, if it decodes a RAM-space address anytime during S2, without waiting for /AS to indicate that the address is valid. Then, if /AS falls before the end of S3, and a RAM-space address is still present, /RAS is generated.

However, the RAM-address multiplexers switch from row addresses to column addresses at the beginning of S4, regardless of when /RAS occurred. If /AS falls later than the first 20 ns of S3, the RAM addresses will change too soon after /RAS, causing RAM errors.

Furthermore, if /AS has not fallen by the end of S3, RAS-Enable is negated, a process that takes the first 20 ns of S4. If /AS falls during that 20 ns, a /RAS spike is generated that can cause RAM errors.

These restrictions mean that, to avoid problems when addressing the Macintosh SE RAM, expansion card logic must never let /AS fall during the period from 20ns into S3 through 20 ns into S4. See Figure 13-3. There is one exception to this: If it is guaranteed that the gate array did not decode a RAM-space address (even on a floating address bus) during S2 or the first 20 ns of S3, then no RAS-Enable is generated, and a RAM-space address and /AS anytime after the first 20 ns of S3 will not cause a /RAS until the usual point in the next RAM-access cycle.

The state machine in the gate array is synchronized to the 15.6672 MHz clock, C16M, from which C8M is derived with a time delay of up to 30 ns. The MC68000 only issues /AS during even-numbered states and is synchronized to the 7.8336 MHz clock, C8M. This difference in timing sources assures that /AS in the Macintosh SE will not occur in the prohibited time interval.

Available address space

The Macintosh SE address map in Figure 13-4 labels which portions of the total address space are currently used by the Macintosh SE hardware (shaded regions). Any address space not used by the Macintosh SE hardware is available for use by an expansion card. There are, of course, some limitations to this:

☐ For any access to the address space $00 0000 through $DF FFFF, the Macintosh SE gate array returns /DTACK in S4, following an address strobe (/AS) in S2. If /AS falls after S3, /DTACK is supplied in S0 of the next access cycle (except for RAM accesses, which wait until S4 of the next cycle). This space is best for fast, asynchronous exchanges.

☐ For an access to the space $E0 0000 through $FF FFFF, the gate array returns /VPA immediately following /AS, and the MC68000 then provides /VMA timed by the E clock. This space is designed for accessing slower, 6800-style synchronous peripherals.

☐ The Macintosh SE RAM, or multiple images of that RAM, always occupy the entire address space $00 0000 through $3F FFFF.

☐ The Macintosh SE does not support the connection of more than one expansion card or device. In particular, no means is provided for arbitrating among multiple external processors, or among cards that use the same address space.

☐ When a Macintosh SE logic board is sent to an Apple service center for repair, Apple's board testing equipment runs test software in address ranges $50 0000 through $51 FFFF and $F8 0000 through $F9 FFFF. Normally, those spaces may be used by an expansion card, as any such card would be removed prior to testing at an Apple service center. However, if a developer expects that customers will leave an expansion card connected to the Macintosh SE logic board when that board is sent to Apple service, such an expansion card should not use the Apple test software spaces.

☐ When servicing an interrupt, the MC68000 reads an address in the range $FF FFF0 through $FF FFFF. The Macintosh SE gate array returns /VPA, causing the processor to ignore any data read and to jump through the appropriate auto-vector location in low memory. The processor does an auto-vector jump only if it reads the address in servicing an interrupt, so this space may be used by an expansion card device if that device will not be confused by auto-vector reads.

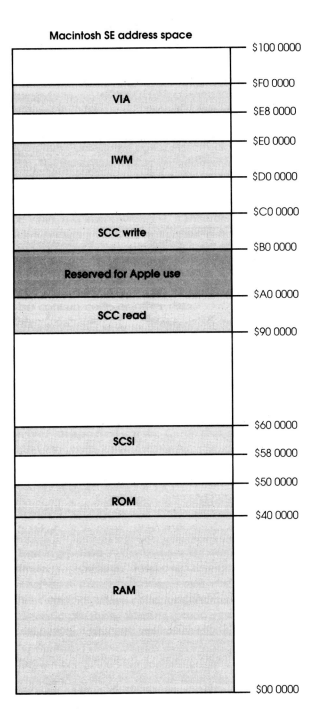

Figure 13-4
Macintosh SE address space

EMI guidelines for expansion cards

The Macintosh SE computer meets FCC electromagnetic interference (EMI) requirements as a stand-alone device, or when connected to a peripheral device such as a printer or modem. However, to avoid exceeding the mandatory FCC limits when your card is added to the Macintosh SE, you should follow certain guidelines while developing your card. The guidelines given in this section apply to an internally mounted card that does not connect to the outside through the accessory access port. If your card connects to the outside, see the additional guidelines in the section "EMI Guidelines for External Connections" in Chapter 15.

The following guidelines should enable you to build an add-on that does not degrade the Macintosh SE to the extent that the combination product does not meet FCC regulations for Class B equipment. However, you are responsible for the FCC authorization of the combination product. Development testing should be undertaken as soon as you have a realistic expansion card, in order to alert you, the developer, to any serious EMI problems. These problems can be resolved by re-routing signal conductors, filtering and bypassing, and eliminating excessive transient ringing (undershoot) on clocks and other signals by providing the proper terminations for buses. Appropriate emission control techniques must be used on the card and on wiring to any connector in the accessory access port.

- Use cards with a minimum of four layers so that separate power planes can reduce EMI emissions from the card.

- Buffer high speed signals and separate them from lower-speed circuitry.

- Buffer signals from the 96-pin connector as close to the connector as possible and limit the drive to one LS load with a maximum of 30 pF capacitance.

- Internal interconnecting cables should be as short as possible. Position cables such that inductive and capacitive coupling with the Macintosh SE subassemblies is minimized.

- Conductors carrying high speed signals should not be bundled with conductors carrying low speed signals. In certain cases, internal shielding or the use of twisted pairs within cables may be required.

- Cards require good high-frequency decoupling in addition to adequate power supply filtering at their low-voltage power connectors. This avoids degrading the low emission levels conducted from the Macintosh SE AC power cord.

Power budget

The Macintosh SE power supply supports the addition of optional Desktop Bus devices, an internal hard disk, and an expansion card. Table 13-3 gives the power budget for these additions.

Table 13-3
Power budget

Macintosh SE device	Amps			
	At +5V	At –5V	At +12V	At –12V
All Apple Desktop Bus devices	0.5	—	—	—
Internal SCSI hard disk	1.5	—	0.9	—
Expansion card[†]	1.5	0.1	0.15	0.1

[†] This is the allotted current for the expansion card, but, for thermal considerations, the total power of the expansion card should not exceed 7 watts.

Regarding the +5V supply, the specification for the 96-pin connector allows 1.5A to be used from all +5V pins combined. This limit is to control the heat dissipated in the restricted space over the Macintosh SE logic board, where an expansion card would be located. An additional 750mA can be used for powering a peripheral device that is located outside of the Macintosh SE case.

Regarding the +12V supply, the specification for the 96-pin connector allows 150mA to be used from all +12V pins combined. Peak surge current up to 1.5A can be tolerated briefly (up to ten seconds), when starting up a disk drive, for example.

Chapter 14

Physical Design Guide for Macintosh SE Cards

This chapter contains physical design guidelines for the development of Macintosh SE expansion cards including

☐ assembly drawings, showing provision for an expansion card

☐ description of the mating 96-pin connectors for expansion card and logic board

☐ heat dissipation guidelines

☐ product safety guidelines

Mechanical drawings

Figures 14-1 through 14-3 show the spatial relationship between a generic expansion card and the Macintosh SE main logic board.

Warning

Figure 14-1 is from a design guide used within Apple Computer and was correct at the time of publication. Future updates may be made available through APDA, the Apple Programmer's and Developer's Association.

You can purchase blank Macintosh SE expansion cards for prototyping from

Diversified I/O, Inc.
1008 Stewart Drive
Sunnyvale, CA 94086
(408) 730-2171
AppleLink Address: D0242

Product name and description:
FreeBus Prototyping Kit, #451104
Board, including SE-Bus connector, supports the expansion slot.

Product name and description:
TwoBus Extender Kit, #450102
Extends prototyping activities beyond the confines of the computer case.
Supports both Macintosh II and Macintosh SE extension.

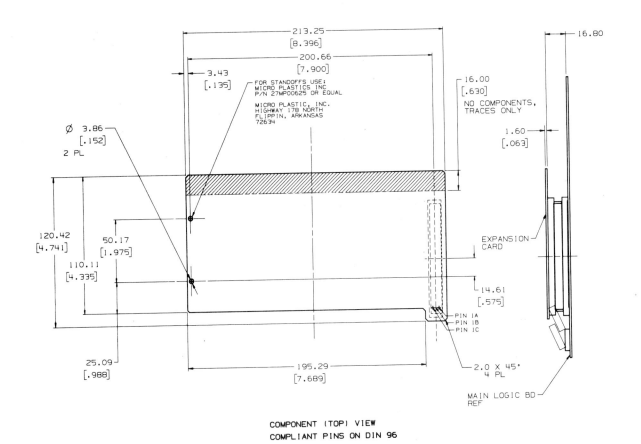

213.25
[8.396]

200.66
[7.900]

3.43
[.135]

FOR STANDOFFS USE:
MICRO PLASTICS INC
P/N 27MP00625 OR EQUAL

MICRO PLASTIC, INC.
HIGHWAY 178 NORTH
FLIPPIN, ARKANSAS
72634

Ø 3.86
[.152]
2 PL

16.00
[.630]
NO COMPONENTS,
TRACES ONLY

1.60
[.063]

120.42
[4.741]

50.17
[1.975]

110.11
[4.335]

EXPANSION
CARD

14.61
[.575]

PIN 1A
PIN 1B
PIN 1C

25.09
[.988]

195.29
[7.689]

2.0 X 45°
4 PL

MAIN LOGIC BD
REF

16.80

COMPONENT (TOP) VIEW
COMPLIANT PINS ON DIN 96

Figure 14-1
Macintosh SE expansion card design guide

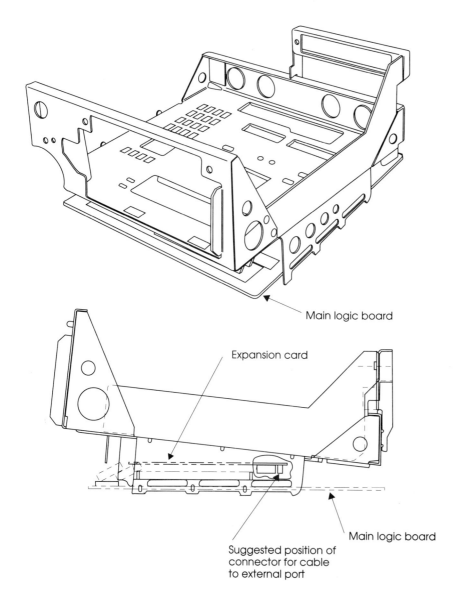

Main logic board

Expansion card

Main logic board

Suggested position of
connector for cable
to external port

Figure 14-2
An expansion card in the Macintosh SE assembly

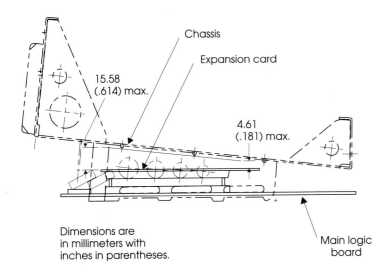

Chassis

Expansion card

15.58
(.614) max.

4.61
(.181) max.

Dimensions are
in millimeters with
inches in parentheses.

Main logic
board

Side view height restrictions

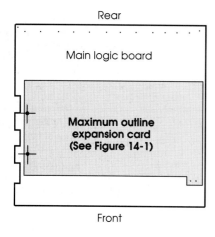

Rear

Main logic board

**Maximum outline
expansion card
(See Figure 14-1)**

Front

Figure 14-3
An expansion card and the main logic board

The 96-pin connector

Figure 14-4 shows a *plug connector* that mates with the Euro-DIN 96-pin *socket connector* on the main logic board. The plug connector should have compliant pins (force fit insertion) rather than solder-type pins for connection to the expansion card if components are to be mounted on the top side of the card.

Figure 14-5 shows the 96-pin socket connector on the main logic board assembly. Figure 14-6 is a detail of the socket connector used on the main logic board.

A source of Euro-DIN connectors meeting Apple specifications is

AMP Incorporated
Harrisburg, PA 17105

Because of high volume production requirements, Apple purchases specially modified versions of the Euro-DIN connector from this vendor. However, you may purchase a mating connector of standard configuration from this or other vendors.

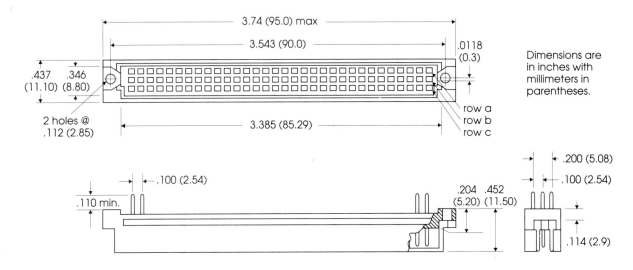

Three-row pin connector

96 contact positions
2.54 mm (.100 inch) spacing pins
Gold plated, 20 microinches, over nickel plate

Figure 14-4
96-pin plug connector for an expansion card

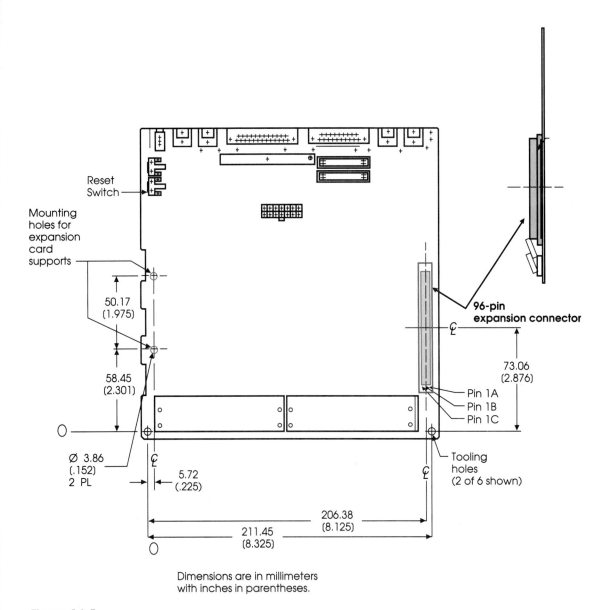

Reset Switch

Mounting holes for expansion card supports

50.17 (1.975)

58.45 (2.301)

Ø 3.86 (.152) 2 PL

5.72 (.225)

96-pin expansion connector

73.06 (2.876)

Pin 1A
Pin 1B
Pin 1C

Tooling holes (2 of 6 shown)

206.38 (8.125)

211.45 (8.325)

Dimensions are in millimeters with inches in parentheses.

Figure 14-5
Connector and mounting suppports for an expansion card

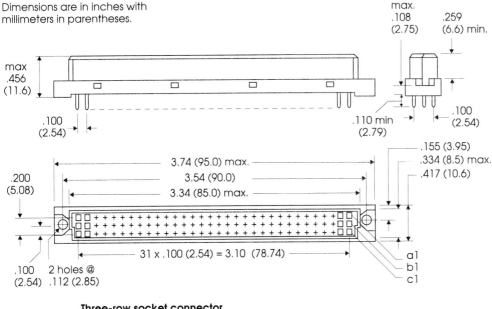

Dimensions are in inches with millimeters in parentheses.

max. .108 (2.75)
.259 (6.6) min.

max .456 (11.6)

.100 (2.54)

.110 min (2.79)

.100 (2.54)

3.74 (95.0) max.
3.54 (90.0)
3.34 (85.0) max.

.155 (3.95)
.334 (8.5) max.
.417 (10.6)

.200 (5.08)

31 x .100 (2.54) = 3.10 (78.74)

a1
b1
c1

.100 (2.54)   2 holes @ .112 (2.85)

Three-row socket connector

96 contact positions
2.54 mm (.100 inch) spacing sockets
Gold plated, 20 microinches, over nickel plate

Figure 14-6
Detail of 96-pin socket connector used on main logic board

Heat dissipation guidelines

Macintosh SE expansion cards, by their own heat dissipation, produce increased temperatures within the Macintosh SE. Because excessive heat can have a detrimental effect on performance and reliability, Apple recommends the following guidelines:

☐ Dissipation by the expansion card of up to 7.5 watts of power provides a comfortable margin for the major Macintosh SE components. Dissipation of more than 7.5 watts of power may cause excessive temperature rise on certain critical components. Apple studies indicate that at an ambient temperature of about 24°C, 7.5 watts of dissipated power from the expansion card will cause an acceptable rise in average component case temperature to about 53°C for the main logic board components located directly under the expansion card (studies conducted with an internal hard disk drive installed).

☐ The most heat-sensitive logic board components include the MC68000 and the DRAM SIMM modules. The maximum recommended temperature for the center of the MC68000 case is 65°C. The maximum recommended temperature for the case of each component on the DRAM SIMM modules is 60°C.

- You can achieve optimum cooling for both the logic board and expansion cards by positioning the expansion card as far above the logic board as possible (without mechanical interference with the chassis); the suggested parameter is 16.8mm. In addition, you will get a more uniform temperature distribution if you place the components on the top rather than the bottom side of the card.

- Put hot components toward the rear of the expansion card, away from the front bezel, to get better cooling by the air flow from the fan.

- An expansion card should not cause the case temperature of an internal hard disk to rise more than 15°C over external ambient air temperature.

- Internally mounted disk drives should not cause the air temperature inside the Macintosh SE case to rise more than 15°C over external ambient air temperature.

- Components placed on a connector board mounted to the accessory access port should cool without significant thermal impact on other Macintosh SE components or parts (particularly the hard disk drive).

Product safety guidelines

The Macintosh SE computer meets national and international product safety requirements. Therefore, any additional cards and components need careful safety consideration to maintain the same degree of electrical and mechanical safety. When you design an expansion card for the Macintosh SE, you must consider several product safety issues.

The Macintosh SE is approved by American (Underwriters Laboratories–UL), Canadian (Canadian Standards Association–CSA), and European (Institute for Industrial Research and Standards–IIRS) regulatory organizations in a configuration without any third-party expansion cards. When you change the design of the product by adding a card, the product becomes delisted. Technically, you should resubmit the Macintosh SE with your card installed and have the new (combination) product evaluated. The new product should have a new model number; the Macintosh SE becomes a component of your system.

You can maintain product safety by following these guidelines:

- Stay within the maximum power specification of the expansion connector.

- Use components that have been certified by the safety agencies. Components such as lithium batteries, power relays, tape drives, wires and cables, and other parts should have at least the UL or CSA approvals.

- [ ] Be careful to maintain proper through-air and over-surface spacings between the high voltage components (power supply, CRT, and so forth) and the logic circuitry. Remember that spacings are measured under worst case conditions and that if a card can be moved, spacings will be measured with the card in the worst position. Spacing tables can be found in the the following safety standards: UL478, CSA 22.2 No. 154-M1983, CSA 22.2 No. 220-M1986, IEC 380, IEC 435, and IEC 950.

- [ ] Maintain proper insulation thickness or layers between the high voltage components and the logic circuitry. (Proper insulation is defined in the standards listed in the preceding item.) If a low voltage circuit can contact a high voltage wire, the low voltage wire must also be insulated for the higher voltage.

- [ ] Properly secure (mount) the components. Avoid mounting that depends on adhesive only or mounting that allows movement of components or cards.

- [ ] Avoid using materials that could contribute to a fire, should one start in the enclosure. These include PCB material, card guides, and other parts. In general, PCB material should be flame rated 94V-1 or better, wire should be UL Listed/CSA Certified, flame rated VW-1, and plastic parts within the enclosure should be flame rated 94V-2 or better.

- [ ] Place PCBs and other components so that they do not block vent openings or fan circulation. Also avoid placement of components next to high voltage parts.

- [ ] Secure all wiring and provide chafing protection to prevent degradation of the insulation on moving parts or sharp edges.

- [ ] Do not allow maintenance work to be performed by persons not knowledgeable of the hazards involved. Repair personnel must be aware of the dangers of shock from the primary, the charge stored in the CRT, and the implosion potential of the CRT.

- [ ] Conversion or installation instructions should be complete. Solicit a review by a person who is unfamiliar with the product to ensure that instructions are complete and accurate enough for that person to understand.

- [ ] Do not configure connectors such that a hazard is created if they are plugged in backwards or into the wrong connector.

- [ ] Avoid splicing of wires. Conversion kits should provide new harnesses if they are required.

- [ ] Avoid soldering. If soldering is necessary, the connection should be made mechanically secure before soldering (no tack soldering).

- [ ] Conversion or installation kits must be complete. Provide any special tools required (for example, a special nut driver). Provide any special hardware rather than expect the installer to modify (bend or drill, for example) existing hardware.

Chapter 15

External Connections
for Macintosh SE Cards

This chapter discusses both electrical and physical considerations required in making connections to external equipment.

The Macintosh SE provides an accessory access port through which another piece of equipment can be connected. Typically, a cable would be routed from the expansion card upward through a slot in the Macintosh SE chassis, and then to a connector on your connector card.

Mechanical drawings in this chapter show the provision Apple has made for connecting your expansion card to devices external to the Macintosh SE.

Mechanical drawings

Figure 15-1 shows the Macintosh SE sheet metal and the structure for mounting your connector and connector card; the recommended cable routing is also shown.

Foldout 4 at the end of the book is a design guide for the connector card. There are two areas of particular note in Foldout 4. It is important that no components, printed wiring traces, or feedthroughs (plated-through-holes) be located in the inner slashed area because contact is made there with the sheet metal of the chassis bracket. The more darkly shaded area may be populated with components no more than 2.0 mm in height.

Warning

Foldout 4 is from a design guide used within Apple Computer and was correct at the time of publication. Future updates may be made available through APDA, the Apple Programmer's and Developer's Association.

EMI guidelines for external connections

Connecting a cable to the accessory access port can seriously compromise the emissions integrity built into the Macintosh SE. Unless you take care during construction and test of *the total system as it will be operated,* you are likely to exceed the allowable limits on conducted and radiated emissions. The total system includes

☐ the unmodified Macintosh SE

☐ the expansion card, the connector card, and all internal cables used to modify the Macintosh SE

☐ the external cable and peripherals to be connected

The guidelines given in Chapter 13 for internal expansion cards also apply to cards that have an external connection. Here are some additional guidelines that apply when you plan to make external connections.

☐ Include EMI filtering in each I/O and power line going to or beyond (outside) the accessory access port connector. This is best achieved by using deglitch packs or common mode chokes on the connector card. Such a card is shown in Foldout 3 at the end of the book.

☐ Shape the spectrum of signals, especially video, in the frequency domain so that unrequired bandwidth and harmonics are not needlessly propagated. (Note: computer designers tend to prefer very fast edges so that timing errors are never a problem, but it is these very fast edges that cause high amplitude harmonics in the frequency domain and lead to emission problems.)

☐ Use a good quality connector, one that has high conductivity (electrical) plating and accepts a shielded plug. The tin-plated steel DB series of connectors is one obvious example. The connector should be mechanically and electrically bonded to the metal chassis behind the aperture at the rear of the Macintosh SE. An unsecured, unbonded connector protruding through the plastic aperture is almost certain to cause a major EMI problem.

☐ External metal conductor cables must be shielded, without exception. Solder bond the entire circumference of the braided shield to provide a low impedance path to the entire perimeter of the connector.

☐ Interconnecting cables should be as short as possible. Conductors carrying high speed signals should not be bundled with conductors carrying low speed signals. In certain cases, you may have to use internal shielding or twisted pairs within cables.

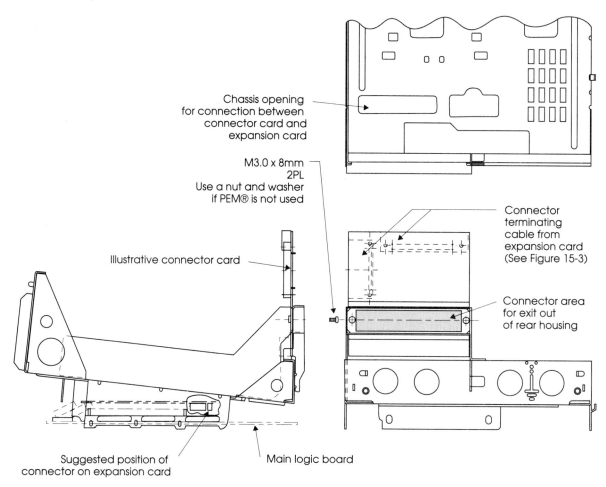

Chassis opening
for connection between
connector card and
expansion card

M3.0 x 8mm
2PL
Use a nut and washer
if PEM® is not used

Illustrative connector card

Connector
terminating
cable from
expansion card
(See Figure 15-3)

Connector area
for exit out
of rear housing

Suggested position of
connector on expansion card

Main logic board

Figure 15-1

Connector card mounting on chassis

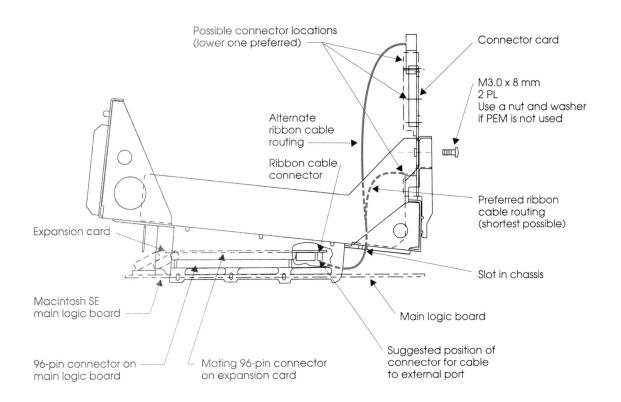

Possible connector locations
(lower one preferred)

Connector card

M3.0 x 8 mm
2 PL
Use a nut and washer
if PEM is not used

Alternate
ribbon cable
routing

Ribbon cable
connector

Preferred ribbon
cable routing
(shortest possible)

Expansion card

Slot in chassis

Macintosh SE
main logic board

Main logic board

96-pin connector on
main logic board

Mating 96-pin connector
on expansion card

Suggested position of
connector for cable
to external port

Chapter 16

Design of a Disk Controller for the Macintosh SE

This chapter contains a performance-proven example of design for the SE-Bus of the Macintosh SE. It describes the electrical and interface characteristics of a simple disk controller card that allows the Macintosh SE processor to communicate with a generic disk drive through the SE-Bus.

The disk controller card allows for one drive to be connected to the Macintosh SE through the cable supplied. The disk controller is inexpensive, but is capable of two software selectable recording formats: FM or MFM. FM is an IBM 3740 compatible, single-density format. MFM is an IBM System 34 compatible, double-density format.

The disk controller card plugs into the 96-pin expansion connector on the main logic board of the Macintosh SE and connects to a floppy disk drive located outside the Macintosh SE. The installation of this card and its associated cables is intended to be done by dealers and not by end users. The disk controller card consists of a disk controller IC and a disk interface IC, a DMA controller IC, some buffers, and three PALs. All controlling firmware and sector-buffering RAM exists in the Macintosh SE.

The control registers are mapped into the address space of the Macintosh SE from $80 0000 through $8F FFFF. No other address space is memory mapped to the controller.

System configuration

The controller package inside the Macintosh SE consists of a disk controller expansion card, a 26-wire flat ribbon cable, and a connector card.

The disk controller card connects to the Macintosh SE processor through the 96-pin expansion connector on the main logic board assembly. A six-inch long ribbon cable ties the disk controller card to the connector card.

The connector card, which mounts to the bracket behind the accessory access port, contains two connectors. One connector is a 26-pin connector, which terminates the six-inch ribbon cable from the internal controller card. The other connector is a DB-37 into which the external disk drive can be plugged via the cable supplied with that drive. See Figure 15-1, Figure 15-2, and Foldout 3 for drawings depicting the configuration.

Interface card block diagram

Figure 16-1 contains a block diagram of the floppy disk controller.

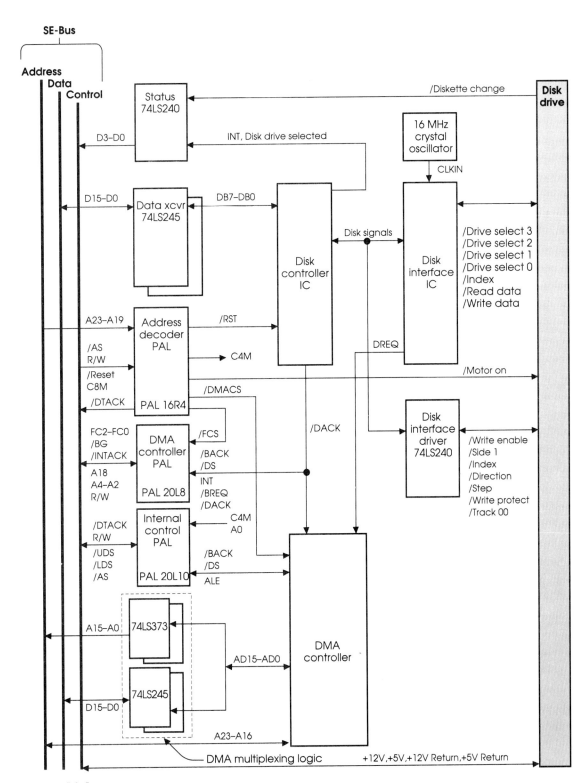

Figure 16-1
Floppy disk controller block diagram

The controller card is made up of the following parts, shown in Figure 16-1:

Control PALs: These PALs provide the address decoding and timing control for the disk controller. They memory map the various control and status registers of the disk controller into the Macintosh SE address space $80 000 through $8F FFFF.

Data bus transceivers: These 74LS245 buffers provide multiplexing control and sufficient current drive to and from the controller onto the data bus. During high-byte transfers, data is placed on D8–D15, while during low-byte transfers, the data goes on D0–D7.

Status driver: The status driver allows three signals to be read by the Macintosh SE: disk selected, disk controller interrupt (INT), and diskette change.

Disk controller IC: This LSI chip contains the circuitry necessary to connect to the generic disk drive. Coupled with the companion disk interface IC chip, it handles all operations with the drive including read and write data, formatting, seeking, sensing drive status, and recalibrating.

Disk interface IC: This chip provides drive and timing support to the disk controller IC. It contains write precompensation and phase-locked loop circuitry.

Disk interface driver: The disk interface driver buffers and provides current drive for several signals coming from and going to the disk drive. It also is used as a multiplexer for four of these signals.

16-MHz crystal clock oscillator: This oscillator provides a 16-MHz clock to the disk interface IC for use in the drive interface.

Dual channel DMA controller and DMA control PAL: The DMA controller handles all DMA data transfer operations between the disk controller IC and the Macintosh SE memory.

DMA address and data multiplexing logic: The dual channel DMA controller has a multiplexed address and data bus. The multiplexing logic is used to demultiplex this bus. The logic consists of two 74LS373's and two 74LS245's.

Floppy disk controller logic

The disk drive control is provided by the disk controller IC, disk interface IC, and some 74LS240 drivers. The disk controller IC is the controlling chip and communicates with the disk interface IC. Details of this logic are not directly relevant to the SE-Bus interface and so will not be given here.

Macintosh SE interface logic

The controller communicates with the SE-Bus via several drivers and PALs. The controller follows the timing of the SE-Bus whether in PIO (programmed input/output) or DMA (direct memory access) transfers.

Certain key signals are described in Table 16-1.

Table 16-1
Bus control signals

Signal name	Signal description
/AS	Indicates a valid address is on the address bus
/UDS	Indicates that valid data is on the data bus D8–D15
/LDS	Indicates that valid data is on the data bus D0–D7
R/W	Defines a cycle to be a read or a write cycle
/DTACK	Signals that the data transfer cycle is completed
/BR	Signals that the controller card would like to own the SE-Bus in order to perform a DMA transfer
/BG	Signals to the controller that it owns the SE-Bus after completion of the current bus cycle
FC0-FC2	These are the MC68000 processor status code and serve to signal an interrupt acknowledge cycle when they are all asserted high
ALE	Signals that the DMA controller is gating a valid address onto the multiplexed address/data lines AD0–AD15
/DS	Signals that data may be moved into or out of the DMA controller on the multiplexed AD0–AD15
/DMACS	Selects the DMA controller during PIO transfers to or from it
BREQ	Indicates that the DMA controller would like to take the SE-Bus
BACK	Indicates that the DMA controller has the SE-Bus
/DREQ	The disk interface IC makes a DMA request to the DMA controller
/DACK	The DMA controller acknowledges the disk interface IC's DMA request
/EOP	Signals that a disk read or write command has been terminated because the data requested has been transferred

Programmed I/O (PIO) operations

All control information is passed to the disk controller and all status information is transferred to the MC68000 using programmed I/O (PIO) transfers (DMA is used for *data* transfer). The MC68000 host initiates the transfer by asserting /AS, R/W, /UDS, and /LDS. Data is then transferred and /DTACK is asserted by the BBU gate array of the Macintosh SE. The PALs decode the address from address lines A18–A23 and thus select either the disk interface IC or the DMA controller to read or write data. Control of the R/W signal determines whether the cycle is a read or a write cycle. See Figure 16-2 for signal timing.

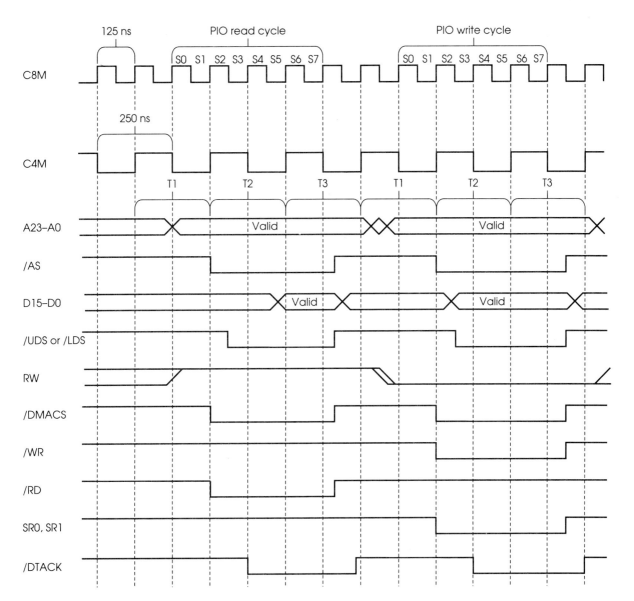

Figure 16-2
Controller PIO timing

DMA operations

All data information is transferred to or from the host (MC68000 or a coprocessor) using DMA transfers. After all control information is written to set up both the disk interface IC and the DMA controller, the DMA operation begins.

The disk controller IC requests each DMA transfer, via the signal /DREQ, and that request is funnelled through the DMA controller and through the PAL control logic. A bus request is then made on the SE-Bus. After the current bus operation has been completed, the MC68000 asserts the signal /BG (bus grant). The PAL logic recognizes /BG and waits for any current bus operation to be completed before it signals the disk controller IC to begin a DMA.

As soon as it has taken over the bus, the DMA controller gates the target DMA address onto the lines AD0–AD15 and the lines A16–A23. See Figure 16-1. Using the signal ALE as a reference, the PAL interface logic latches the address from AD0–AD15 with the signal /ADDR. Because all DMA data transfer operations must be sychronized to the signal /PMCYC (processor memory cycle), the PALs wait for /PMCYC to go low, inserting wait states in the transfer cycle of the DMA controller.

❖ *Note:* /PMCYC is the signal used to synchronize all SE-Bus activity. The disk controller waits for /PMCYC to go low before beginning a bus cycle. The signals /AS, /UDS, /LDS, and R/W are not asserted until /PMCYC goes low. The memory timing of the Macintosh SE is synchronized to /PMCYC. See Figure 13-2 in Chapter 13. The disk controller is designed to present timing as similar to the MC68000 as possible during a bus cycle (/PMCYC low). /PMCYC goes high during state zero (S0) of the MC68000 timing and during video memory accesses.

The PALs then assert /AS, /UDS, /LDS, and R/W after gating the address onto the address bus. If a processor read operation (processor reading from the disk interface card) is requested, the PALs gate the data to the correct byte of the data bus from the disk interface IC and generate the proper disk controller read signal. If a processor write operation (processor writing to the the disk interface card) is requested, the PALs turn on the correct transceiver to write the data and assert the proper write signal to the disk controller IC.

Address allocation

The disk controller card's device select space ranges from $80 0000 through $8F FFFF and is divided up into four blocks. From $80 0000 through $83 FFFF the main status register within the disk controller can be read. A write to this address turns on the signal RST (resets the disk controller). From $84 0000 through $87 FFFF, control, status, and data information may be read from or written to the disk controller data register. Writing in the area $88 0000 through $8B FFFF turns on the drive motor; reading in this area turns both the motor and RST off. The DMA controller is read to or written from via the addressing range $8C 0000 through $8F FFFF. See Table 16-2.

Table 16-2
Device select decode addresses

Decode address range	Device selected and action resulting
$80 0000–$83 FFFF	Read from main status register of disk controller IC. A write to this address turns RST on (resets the disk controller IC). Also, read additional status register. The main status register is on the least significant byte and the additional status register is on the most significant.
$84 0000–$87 FFFF	Read or write control, status, and data information to the data register in the disk controller IC.
$88 0000–$8B FFFF	Write turns drive motor to on, read turns motor and controller's reset signal off. (Interrupts are enabled when the motor is on!)
$8C 0000–$8F FFFF	Read from or write to DMA controller.

Data is normally read from and written to the disk controller card with MC68000 MOVE.B instructions. Additional status information may be obtained by reading anywhere in the addressing range $80 0000 through $83 FFFF using MOVE.W instructions.

The status register within the disk controller IC may be read with a MOVE.B instruction in the address range $80 0000 through $83 FFFF.

The data register within the disk controller IC may be read or written with a MOVE.B instruction in the address range $84 0000 through $87 FFFF. It is through the data register that commands, data, and the contents of status registers 0 through 3 are passed. Any disk operation is initiated by passing the several commands required to the disk controller IC via this register.

The read track operation allowed by the disk controller IC is supported on this disk controller. After the execute portion of any operation is completed, the disk controller IC may give back status information in status registers 0 through 3.

Additional status information may be read with a MOVE.W instruction in the address space $80 0000 through $83 FFFF.

The DMA controller is given commands via the chain control table that exists in Macintosh SE RAM. The address of this table is loaded into the chain address register before a chain load command is given to the DMA controller. The chain control table consists of values needed by the DMA controller to transfer data.

The DMA controller will, upon receiving a chain load command, load its registers from the chain control table. After the registers are loaded, the DMA controller is ready to transfer data. Data transfers are then initiated, byte by byte, by the disk controller IC.

Appendix A

PAL Listings for the NuBus Test Card

This is a listing of the PAL implemented logic equations for the NuBus Test Card described in Chapter 10, "Design Examples."

```
.ident   PAL16R8,B   SLAVE, NuBus slave controller

         Version:    1.1

.names

                /CLK
        /START  /ACK  /MYSLOT  /RESET  /MSTDN  /TM1  A19D11  A18D10
                Gnd  /OE
        A18D10L  A19D11L  TM1L  MASTER  /romoe1  /ROMOE  /ACKCY  SLAVE
                Vcc

.equations

    /SLAVE        :=  RESET
                          {initialization}
                  +  /SLAVE * /START
                  +  /SLAVE * ACK
                  +  /SLAVE * /MYSLOT
                          {holding;  DeMorgan of START * /ACK * MYSLOT}
                  +   SLAVE * ACKCY
                          {clearing term}
                  ;

    /MASTER       :=  RESET
                          {initialization}
                  +  /MASTER * /SLAVE
                  +  /MASTER * /TM1L
                  +  /MASTER * /A19D11L
                  +  /MASTER *  A18D10L
                          {holding term;  DeMorgan of:
                              SLAVE * TM1L * A19D11L * /A18D10L }
                  +   MASTER *  MSTDN
                          {clearing term, at end of MASTER cycle}
                  ;

    ROMOE         :=  START * /ACK * MYSLOT * /TM1 * A19D11 * A18D10
                      * /RESET
                          { latching term, when decoding a READ to us }
                  +   ROMOE * /ACKCY
                      * /RESET
                          { holding term thru access }
                  ;
    romoe1        :=  ROMOE
                          { simply a delayed ROMOE for cycle timing }
                  ;
```

```
ACKCY         :=  START * /ACK * MYSLOT * TM1
                      {fast cycle for WRITES}
              +   /ACKCY * SLAVE * /ROMOE
                      {slow cycle for non-ROM READS}
              +   /ACKCY * ROMOE * romoe1 * /A19D11L
                      {slower cycle for ROM }
              ;


/TM1L         :=   RESET
              +   /TM1  *  START * /ACK * MYSLOT
                      {setting term, during address cycle}
              +   /TM1L * /START
              +   /TM1L *            ACK
              +   /TM1L *                    /MYSLOT
                      {holding terms}
              ;


/A19D11L      :=  /A19D11  * START * /ACK * MYSLOT    * /MASTER
                      {setting term, during SLAVE address cycle}
              +   /A19D11L * SLAVE * /TM1L
              +   /A19D11L * SLAVE *  TM1L * /A19D11L
              +   /A19D11L * SLAVE *  TM1L *             A18D10L
                      {holding terms for SLAVE accesses}
              +   ROMOE * romoe1
                      { timing term for ROM reads }
              +   /A19D11  * SLAVE *  TM1L *  A19D11L * /A18D10L
                      {setting term for MASTER start}
              +   /A19D11L * MASTER
                      {holding term for MASTER}
              ;


/A18D10L      :=  /A18D10  *  START * /ACK * MYSLOT
                      {setting term, during address cycle}
              +   /A18D10L * SLAVE * /TM1L
              +   /A18D10L * SLAVE *  TM1L * /A19D11L
              +   /A18D10L * SLAVE *  TM1L *             A18D10L
                      {holding terms for SLAVE accesses}
              +   /A18D10  * SLAVE *  TM1L *  A19D11L * /A18D10L
                      {setting term for MASTER start}
              +   /A18D10L * MASTER
                      {holding term for MASTER}
              ;

.notes

     This version corresponds to the new pin-out for the "official"
  test card.  It also supports the ROM, with the ROMOE signal.

.end
```

```
.ident   PAL16L8,B    (ARB2), Nubus Arbitration logic

         Version:    1.1

.names

         nc1  /ARB  nc3 nc4 nc5  /ID3  /ID2  /ID1  /ID0
             gnd
         /ARB0i /ARB0o /ARB1 /ARB2 /ARB3 arb0oe arb1oe arb2oe GRANT
             vcc

.equations

    .if[ ARB * ID3 ]
       ARB3    = VCC;

       /arb2oe = /ID3 * ARB3
               ;
    .if[ ARB * arb2oe * ID2 ]
       ARB2    = VCC;

       /arb1oe = /ID3 * ARB3
               + /ID2 * ARB2
               ;
    .if[ ARB * arb1oe * ID1 ]
       ARB1    = VCC;

       /arb0oe = /ID3 * ARB3
               + /ID2 * ARB2
               + /ID1 * ARB1
               ;
    .if[ ARB * arb0oe * ID0 ]
       ARB0o   = VCC;

       /GRANT  = /ID3 * ARB3
               + /ID2 * ARB2
               + /ID1 * ARB1
               + /ID0 * ARB0i
               ;

.notes

        ARB is responsible for doing the NuBus arbitration logic.  Upon
    detecting any higher priority ARB<3:0> value, it will defer its
    generation of lower ARB<3:0> bits.
        The GRANT signal must be timed externally to determine proper
    NuBus constraints.
        This version uses a new technique to minimize skews.

.end
```

```
.ident   PAL16R8,B   MASTER2, NuBus master controller for test card.

         Version:    1.3

.names

             /CLK
         MASTER  GRANT  /RQST  /START  /ACK  MASTERD  /RESET  A17D9
             gnd  /oe
         A17D9L  /LOCKED  /arbdn  /busy  /OWNER  /DTACY  /ADRCY  /ARBCY
             vcc

.equations

     ARBCY        := MASTER * MASTERD * /OWNER * /ARBCY * /ADRCY * /DTACY *
                     /RQST
                              {wait for RQST* unsserted, while idle}
                  +  MASTER *  ARBCY * /OWNER
                   * /RESET
                              {non-locking, hold for START*}
                  +  MASTER *  ARBCY *  LOCKED
                   * /RESET
                              {holding for locked access}
                  ;
     ADRCY        := /A17D9L * /OWNER * ARBCY * arbdn * GRANT * /busy * /START
                  +  /A17D9L * /OWNER * ARBCY * arbdn * GRANT *  busy *  ACK
                              {START* if not locking}
                  +           OWNER * LOCKED * /ADRCY * /DTACY
                   * MASTER * /RESET
                              {START* for locking case, after LOCK-ATTN}
                  ;
     DTACY        :=  ADRCY
                              {assert after START*}
                  +   DTACY * /ACK
                   * MASTER * /RESET
                              {hold until ACK*}
                  ;
     OWNER        :=  ARBCY * arbdn * GRANT * /busy * /START
                  +   ARBCY * arbdn * GRANT *  busy *  ACK
                              {when bus is free, we own it next}
                  +   OWNER *  ADRCY
                   * MASTER * /RESET
                              {hold before DTACY}
                  +   OWNER *  DTACY * /ACK
                   * MASTER * /RESET
                              {non-locking, wait until ACK*}
                  +   OWNER * LOCKED
                   * MASTER * /RESET
                              {for LOCKing case, hold for NULL-ATTN}
                  ;
```

```
busy          := /busy * START * /ACK
                          {beginning of transaction}
              +   busy *            /ACK
               * /RESET
                          {hold during cycle}
              ;
arbdn         := ARBCY */START
                          {when arbitrating, force delay}
              ;
LOCKED        := A17D9L * ARBCY * arbdn * GRANT * /busy * /START
              +   A17D9L * ARBCY * arbdn * GRANT *  busy *  ACK
                          {set for LOCK-ATN}
              +   LOCKED * /DTACY
               * MASTER * /RESET
              +   LOCKED *  DTACY * /ACK
               * MASTER * /RESET
                          {clear on NULL-ATN}
              ;
/A17D9L       := /A17D9  * /MASTER
                          {latching term}
              +  /A17D9L *  MASTER
                          {holding term}
              +   LOCKED
                          {clearing term, prevent another ADRCY}
              ;
```

.notes

    This version is for new pin-out of the "official" test card.
MasterA handles the delayed feature of the card. Version 1.1 also
fixes the timing for arbitration.
    This version is designed to work with the new ARB2 arbitration
PAL, which has a different sense for GRANT. It also fixes a minor
timing overhang on DTACY for 2-cycle transactions.
    Version 1.3 fixes 2-cycle write by only allowing ADRCY for
1 clock; we originally had overlap to try to eliminate decoding
glitches.

.end

```
.ident   PAL16L8,B   MISC2, local bus/transceiver controls.

         Version:    1.2

.names

         CLK SLAVE TM1L A19D11L A18D10L /ARBCY /ADRCY /DTACY /ROMOE
             gnd
         MASTER  GAB210 /GBA CAB  /DOE  /AOE  /DCLK  /ACLK  GAB3
             vcc


.equations

    GBA          =  SLAVE * /TM1L
                              {SLAVE read of card}
                 +  MASTER * ADRCY
                              {MASTER address cycle}
                 +  MASTER * DTACY * A19D11L{TM1}
                              {MASTER data cycle, when writing}
                 ;
    /CAB         =  SLAVE + /CLK
                              { DeMorgan of:  /SLAVE * CLK }
                 ;
    /GAB3        =  SLAVE * /TM1L
                              {any SLAVE read}
                 +  MASTER * /ADRCY * /DTACY
                              {MASTER loading address}
                 +  MASTER * A19D11L{TM1}
                              {MASTER write}
                 ;
    /GAB210      =  SLAVE * /TM1L * /ROMOE
                              {SLAVE, non-ROM, read}
                 +  MASTER * /ADRCY * /DTACY
                              {MASTER loading address}
                 +  MASTER * A19D11L{TM1}
                              {MASTER write}
                 ;
    ACLK         =  SLAVE * CLK *  TM1L * /A19D11L * /A18D10L
                    * /ROMOE
                              {SLAVE write to address reg}
                 ;

    AOE          =  SLAVE *        /TM1L * /A19D11L * /A18D10L
                    * /ROMOE
                              {SLAVE read of address reg}
                 +  MASTER * /ADRCY * /DTACY
                              {MASTER address cycle}
                 ;
```

```
DCLK        =  SLAVE * CLK *  TM1L * /A19D11L *  A18D10L
               * /ROMOE
                        {SLAVE write to data reg}
            +  MASTER *  DTACY *      /A19D11L{/TM1} *    CLK
                        {MASTER read}
            ;

DOE         =  SLAVE *       /TM1L * /A19D11L *  A18D10L
               * /ROMOE
                        {SLAVE read of data reg}
            +  MASTER *  DTACY *      A19D11L{TM1}
                        {MASTER write data}
            ;
```

.notes

     This version of PAL corresponds to the "official" NuBus
test card. Version 1.2 reflects non-overlap of ADRCY with
DTACY, which fixes problem with 2-cycle writes;

.end

```
.ident   PAL16L8,B        NBDRVR2, NuBus bus driver.

        Version:    1.3

.names
    /ACKCY /ARBCY /ADRCY /DTACY /OWNER /LOCKED nc7 A19D11L A18D10L
        Gnd
    nc11 /TM0 /TM1 /tmoe /MSTDN /rqstoe /ACK   START /RQST
        Vcc


.equations

        rqstoe   =  ARBCY * /ADRCY
                             {hold until START* for normal case}
                 +  ARBCY *  LOCKED
                             {hold until NULL-ATTN for locked case}
 '                     ;
    .if[ rqstoe ]
        RQST     =  Vcc;

    .if[ OWNER ]
        START    = /DTACY
                             {START* for all non-DTA cycles}
                     ;

        tmoe     =  ACKCY
                             {SLAVE response}
                 +  OWNER *  ARBCY * /DTACY
                             {we own bus, while not waiting for ACK}
                     ;
    .if[ tmoe ]
        ACK      =  ACKCY
                             {SLAVE response}
                 +  OWNER * /ADRCY
                             {for NULL-ATTN, LOCK-ATTN}
                     ;

    .if[ tmoe ]
        TM1      =  ACKCY
                             {SLAVE response}
                 +  OWNER *  ADRCY * A19D11L
                             {START* at address cycle}
                 +  OWNER * /ADRCY * /LOCKED
                             {set for NULL-ATTN}
                     ;
```

```
    .if[ tmoe ]
        TM0     =   ACKCY
                            {SLAVE response}
                +   OWNER *  ADRCY * A18D10L
                            {START* at address cycle}
                +   OWNER *  /ADRCY
                            {always set for xxxx-ATTN cycles}

                ;

        MSTDN   =   OWNER * /LOCKED *              DTACY * ACK
                            {done at tail end of normal cycle}
                +   OWNER * /LOCKED * ARBCY * /ADRCY * /DTACY
                            {done for locked cases}

                ;
```

.notes

     This version corresponds to the "offical" test card.
     NOTE: due to overlap of states, RQST* is held one state too
long at end of a LOCKED transaction. However, this causes no "real"
problem. If we are the last winner of a RQST set, then the only
result is that new RQST-ers are held off by one CLK. If there is
another RQST-er left in our set, then it will still be driving RQST.
It will properly arbitrate due to the NULL-ATTENTION and become the
next winner. Thus, in either case, nothing "bad" happens.
     Version 1.3 reflects change to ADRCY which is now held low only
during the address cycle of a transaction.

.end

Appendix B

PAL Listings for the
SCSI-NuBus Test Card

This is a listing of the PAL implemented logic equations for the SCSI NuBus Test Card described in Chapter 10, "Design Examples."

```
.ident  PAL16R8,B   stNUBUS1, control for NuBus SCSI test card.

        Version:    1.1

.names

      clk
    /START  /ACK  /mySLOT  /mySUPER  /TM1  nc7 nc8  /RESET
      gnd  /oe
    nc12  nc13 nc14  /S2  /S1  /SUPER  /SLOT  /IOR
      vcc


.equations

    IOR      :=  START * /ACK * mySLOT  * /TM1   * /RESET
             +   START * /ACK * mySUPER * /TM1   * /RESET
                       { set on READ to our SLOT }
             +   IOR * /S2                       * /RESET
                       { hold until end of transaction }
             ;

    SLOT     :=  START * /ACK * mySLOT          * /RESET
                       { select when access to us }
             +   SLOT * /S2                     * /RESET
                       { hold thruout cycle }
             ;
    SUPER    :=  START * /ACK * mySUPER         * /RESET
                       { select when access to us }
             +   SUPER * /S2                    * /RESET
                       { hold thruout cycle }
             ;
    S1       :=  SLOT  * /S1                    * /RESET
             +   SUPER * /S1                    * /RESET
             +   S1 * /S2                       * /RESET
             ;
    S2       :=  S1 * /S2                       * /RESET
             ;

.notes

        stNUBUS1 is the main control circuit of the NuBus SCSI card.
    This version will decode both a SuperSlot and a normal Slot access.
    Notice that all bus transactions take the same time to simplify
    the logic.

.end
```

```
.ident    PAL16L8,B    stNUBUS2, control for NuBus SCSI test card.

        Version:    1.0

.names

        /CLK   nc2   /SLOT   /SUPER   /S1   /S2   nc7   DRQ   IRQ
            gnd
        /INTENB   /NMRQ   nc13   /ackoe   /TM0   /TM1   /ACK   DCLK   ACLK
            vcc

.equations

        /ACLK    =    SLOT
                 +    SUPER
                 +    /CLK
                        { DeMorgan of CLK * /(SLOT + SUPER) }
                 ;
        /DCLK    =    /S2
                        { clock in data on edge of ACK* }
                 ;
        ackoe    =    SLOT
                 +    SUPER
                        { try to pull ACK* up before undriving }
                 ;
    .if[   ackoe   ]
        ACK      =    S2
                 ;
    .if[   ackoe   ]
        TM1      =    S2
                 ;
    .if[   ackoe   ]
        TM0      =    S2
                 ;
                        { assert ACK*, TM1*, TM0* during last state of cycle }
    .if[   INTENB   ]
        NMRQ     =    IRQ
                 +    DRQ
                        { drive NMRQ if either is ready }
                 ;

.notes

        This PAL is driven by stNUBUS1 (which provides decoding and timing);
    it generates the control signals used by the NuBus interface.

.end
```

```
.ident   PAL16L8,B    stMISC, control for NuBus SCSI test card.

         Version:    1.0

.names

         /SLOT  /SUPER  /S1  /S2  A19  A18  A9  TM1L  nc9
            gnd
         /RESET  /IOW  nc13 nc14  /INTENB  /RAMCS  /ROMCS  /DACK  /SCSI
            vcc

.equations

         SCSI   =   SLOT * /A19 * /A18 * /A9        * /RESET
                ;
         DACK   =   SLOT * /A19 * /A18 *  A9        * /RESET
                ;
         ROMCS  =   SLOT *  A19 *  A18              * /RESET
                ;
         RAMCS  =   SUPER                           * /RESET
                ;
         INTENB =   SLOT *  A19 * /A18 *  A9        * /RESET
                +   INTENB * /SLOT                  * /RESET
                +   INTENB * /A19                   * /RESET
                +   INTENB *  A18                   * /RESET
                +   INTENB *  A9                    * /RESET
                ;
         IOW    =   SLOT  *  TM1L * /S2
                +   SUPER *  TM1L * /S2
                ;
```

.notes

> This PAL actually generates the selects and R/W strobes to the
> chips on the SCSI test card. stNUBUS1 does the basic slot decoding
> and cycle timing. We simply drive the signals based upon its
> information.
>   Note that we create our own latch for INTENB. S2 behaves like
> the strobe signal; the addresses will stay around after S2 goes away.

.end

Glossary

acknowledge cycle: For the NuBus: Last period of a transaction during which /ACK is asserted by a slave responding to a master. Often shortened to *ack cycle*.

address: A number used to identify a location in the computer's address space. Some locations are allocated to memory, others to I/O devices.

address bus: The path along which the addresses of specific memory locations are transmitted. The width of the path determines how many addresses can be accessed (addressed) directly by the computer. For an n-bit wide address bus, the computer can make use of 2^n locations in memory where information can be stored. In the Macintosh II, for example, the 32-bit address bus permits the processor to access 2^{32} (4.3 billion) addresses. This is more than 250 times as many addresses as computers with a 24-bit bus (or the Macintosh II in 24-bit mode) can access (2^{24} = 16 million).

address space: A range of accessible memory.

AMU (Address Mapping Unit): For the Macintosh II: A custom integrated circuit that allows an operating system to quickly reconfigure the arrangement of memory without physically moving data. Different tasks can be "swapped" within the same space.

arbitration contest: The mechanism used to choose which of two or more cards requesting control of the bus will become the next bus master. For the Macintosh II: The arbitration contest requires two bus periods (at 100 μs each).

asserted: Indicates that a signal is active or true, independent of whether that logical condition is represented by a high or low voltage. For example, in the Macintosh II the signal /RESET is an open-collector, two-state line pulled high by the bus termination unless driven low (asserted) by the line driver; assertion causes NuBus cards to be returned to their power-on state. The signal /TM1 is a three-state line that must be driven from a high impedance, indeterminate voltage level to a high (unasserted, H) level or to a low (asserted, L) level; this line is asserted during the start cycle of a write transaction.

assertion edge: The clock edge on which assertion of synchronous signals takes place.

attention cycle: The name given to a particular kind of start cycle, one in which both /START and /ACK are asserted. There are two types: attention-resource-lock and attention-null cycles.

BIU (bus interface unit): For the Macintosh II: The electronics connecting the MC68020 bus to the NuBus.

block transfer: For the Macintosh II: A transaction that consists of a start cycle, multiple data cycles from or to sequential address locations, and an acknowledge cycle. The number of data cycles is controlled by the bus master and is communicated during the start cycle.

Board sResource list: The sResource list that describes the board in whose declaration ROM the list resides.

bus: A path along which information is transmitted electronically within a computer. Buses connect short-distance networks of computer devices, such as processors, expansion cards, and physical RAM; information that travels along the bus is transmitted according to a set of rules known as a *protocol.*

bus driver: The power output transistor and circuitry used to drive the input impedance of the bus, including the parallel loads of cards connected to the bus.

busy: The bus is busy between start and acknowledge cycles.

bus lock: A mechanism for providing continuing tenure (bus ownership) by a single card. The extended tenure may include multiple transactions or attention cycles. One type of attention cycle is called a *resource lock,* therefore a bus lock may or may not include a resource lock.

bus specification: Describes the physical characteristics of the bus and the protocol that governs the use of the bus. For example, the NuBus specification defines the clock rate of the bus, the width of the bus (in bits), the maximum rate of information transfer, and so on. It also defines the protocol, or the set of commands used to transfer information among the devices using the bus. Therefore, understanding the specification for a bus, like the NuBus architecture implemented in the Macintosh II, can lead to a better understanding of how the entire computer performs.

byte lane: Any of four bytes that make up the NuBus data width. NuBus slot cards may use any or all of the byte lanes to communicate with each other or with the Macintosh II.

byte swapping: The process by which the order of bytes in each 4-byte NuBus word is changed to conform to the byte order of certain processors.

card: A printed circuit board or card connected to the bus in parallel with other cards. Also called a *device* or a *module.*

card-generic driver: A driver that is designed to work with a variety of plug-in cards.

card-specific driver: A driver that is designed to work with a single model of plug-in card.

coprocessor: For the Macintosh II: Any microprocessors on NuBus expansion cards; that is, any microprocessors in addition to the MC68020 on the main logic board. For the Macintosh SE: Any microprocessors on an SE-Bus expansion card; that is, any microprocessors on the SE-Bus in addition to the MC68000 on the main logic board. The term as used in this book is *not* limited to a closely coupled processor such as the MC68881 Floating-Point Coprocessor, also referred to as an accelerator.

Generally, closely coupled coprocessors handle tasks that could be performed by the main processor running appropriate software, but which would be performed much more slowly that way. In contrast, main processors are designed to perform a great variety of tasks, so their construction must be very general. Coprocessor architectures may favor a certain set of operations, like floating point calculations for graphics instruction looping, and therefore they can optimize the speed at which such operations are processed. Other coprocessors perform main system tasks like running alternative operating systems.

CPU (central processing unit): *See* **processor.**

cycle: For the Macintosh II: One period of the NuBus clock, nominally 100 ns in duration and beginning at the rising edge. For the Macintosh SE: One period of the SE-Bus clock.

data bus: The path along which general information is transmitted within the computer. The wider the data bus, the more information can be transmitted at once. The Macintosh II, for example, has a 32-bit data bus. Thus, 32 bits of information can be transferred at a time, so that information is transferred twice as fast as in 16-bit computers (assuming equal system clock rates). The Macintosh SE has 24-bit address and 16-bit data buses within the SE-Bus.

data cycle: Any period in which data is known to be valid and acknowledged. It includes acknowledge cycles as well as intermediate data cycles within a block transfer.

declaration ROM: A ROM on a NuBus slot card that contains information about the card and may also contain code or other data.

DIP switches: Multiple single or double-throw switches in a dual in-line package.

DMA: Direct memory access.

drive: The action of a card when it causes a bus signal line to be in a known, determinate state.

driver-supported cards: Cards that are accessed indirectly via a software driver.

driving edge: The rising edge (low to high) of the central system clock (/CLK).

firmware: Programs permanently stored in ROM.

floating point: A mathematical notation that is similar to scientific notation. Generally, processors that use floating-point notation do their work in binary code, not decimal. Like scientific notation, floating point represents numbers as combinations of mantissas and exponents. For example, in scientific notation, the number 324.63 is represented as 3.2463×10^2, where the 3.2463 part is called the mantissa, and the power to which ten is raised (2) is the exponent. In binary floating-point notation, however, the mantissa is always a binary fraction and the exponent is a power of 2, not 10. The

advantage of using floating point is that, like scientific notation, it permits much larger and smaller numbers to be manipulated than a fixed-point notation could. This wider range of numbers is necessary for computation in many fields, including science, engineering, finance, and graphics. The Macintosh has exceptionally high-quality floating-point performance; in the Macintosh II, the 68881 coprocessor maintains that high quality and speeds up some numerical operations by 200 times.

format block: A structure in a declaration ROM that provides a standard entry point for other structures in the ROM.

frame buffer: A buffer memory in which is stored all the picture elements (pixels) of a frame of video information.

Frame Buffer Controller (FBC): A register-controlled CMOS gate array used to generate and control video data and timing signals.

FPU: Abbreviation for Floating Point Unit.

gamma table: A table that compensates for nonlinearities in a monitor's color response.

geographical addressing: A method of identifying the physical location of a card on the NuBus by having four pins of each connector electrically wired to provide a one-of-sixteen code to each slot connector ($9 through $E for the Macintosh II). A card inserted into a slot connector then has the code for that slot applied to its /ID3–/ID0 lines, without any manual setting of configuration switches as required in some bus systems.

GLU: Acronym for *general logic unit,* a class of custom integrated circuits used as interfaces between different parts of the computer.

halfword: An element of information half the length of a 32-bit word, therefore, 16-bits long.

heap: The area of memory in which space is dynamically allocated and released on demand, using the Memory Manager.

high: For an active-low signal, synonymous with inactive, deasserted, unasserted, false, and released.

inactive: For an active-low signal, synonymous with high.

intelligent card: A card containing one or more processors that can work independently from the main processor of the computer. Intelligent cards can serve as a medium for introducing new processor technologies into a system, but most personal computer bus architectures require too much support from the main processor for this to happen. NuBus, however, is a notable exception, because it was designed specifically to support multiple processors, and hence, intelligent cards.

low: For an active-low signal, synonymous with active and asserted.

master: A card that initiates the addressing of another card or the processor on the main logic board. The card addressed is at that time acting as a slave.

modulo: The integer N measured *modulo 4* will be the remainder (0, 1, 2, or 3) from division of N by 4.

multiplex: To encode information so that fewer wires are needed to transmit it, and the same cable wires and connector pins can transmit different kinds of information. The NuBus multiplexes information so that 32-bit address and data communication can be performed using a single 96-pin connector and still have adequate pins available for other necessary functions. Specifically, 32 pins are used to transmit a memory address and the same 32 pins (at a different time) to transmit data.

null cycle: A type of attention cycle.

open collector: A bus driver that drives a line low or doesn't drive it at all.

PAL: An integrated circuit implementing programmable array logic.

parked: A NuBus master that has released /RQST is parked on the bus until another card asserts /RQST.

peer cards: Cards that are designed to execute code that is not specialized to the card; for example, two cards that are executing cooperating processes to solve a problem.

period: The 100 ns period of /CLK consisting of a 75 ns high state and a 25 ns low state.

PIO (programmed input/output): An interfacing technique where the processor directly accesses registers assigned to I/O devices by executing processor instructions. Memory mapped I/O port registers are addressed as memory locations.

processor: Same as CPU, where the term *central* processing unit may not be literally applicable. The processor contains an arithmetic and logic unit (ALU) and system control hardware. In Macintosh II and Macintosh SE systems containing expansion cards, there may be two or more processors (or CPUs), with none being more central in function than the others; these are multiprocessor systems.

release: To do the opposite of **drive** to a signal line.

released: For an active-low signal, synonymous with high, inactive, deasserted, unasserted, and false.

sampling edge: The falling edge (high to low) of the central system clock.

scaled pixel clock period: A normalizing parameter used in the description of video card operation. One scaled pixel clock period equals 16 times the ratio of pixel clock period to the pixel depth (in bits per pixel).

SCSI (Small Computer System Interface): An industry standard parallel bus that provides a consistent method of connecting computers and peripherals.

SCSI devices: Devices, such as hard disks and tape backup units, that use the Small Computer Systems Interface.

slave: A card that responds to being addressed by another card acting as a master. The Macintosh II main logic board is a card that may be either master or slave. Some cards may be slave-only in function because they lack the circuitry to arbitrate in a bus ownership contest.

slot: (1) A connector attached to the bus. A card may be inserted into any of the physical slots when more than one is provided (the Macintosh II provides six slots). (2) A region in address space (**slot space**) allocated to a physical slot.

slot ID: The hex number corresponding to each card slot. For the Macintosh II: Each slot ID is established by the main logic board of the Macintosh II and communicated to the card through the /IDx lines.

Slot Manager: A set of Macintosh II ROM routines that let applications access declaration ROMs on slot cards.

slot space: The upper one sixteenth of the total address space. These addresses are in the form $Fsxx xxxx where F, s, and x are hex digits of 4 bits each. This address space is geographically divided among the NuBus slots according to slot ID number.

sResource: A software structure in the declaration ROM of a slot card.

sResource directory: The structure in a declaration ROM that provides access to its sResource lists.

sResource list: A list of characteristics of a slot resource.

stack: The area of memory in which space is allocated and released in LIFO (last-in-first-out) order.

start cycle: The first period of a transaction during which /START is asserted. The start cycle is one bus clock period long; the address and transfer type are valid during this cycle.

super slot space: The large portion of memory in the range $9000 0000 through $EFFF FFFF. NuBus addresses of the form $sxxx xxxx (that is, $s000 0000 through $sFFF FFFF) reference the super slot space that belongs to the card in slot s, where s is an ID digit in the range $9 through $E.

tenure: A time period of unbroken bus ownership by a single master. A master may lock the bus and, during one tenure, perform several transactions.

transaction: A complete NuBus operation such as read or write. In the Macintosh II a transaction is made up of an address cycle, wait cycles as required by the responding card, and a data cycle Address cycles are one clock period long and convey address and command information. Data cycles are also one clock period long and convey data and acknowledgement information.

timeout period: The time period that a bus master waits for a non-responding slave to respond before generating a bus timeout error code.

transfer mode: One of the 16 modes or encodings that specify which part of the addressed 32-bit word is to be transferred.

three-state: A bus driver that drives a line low or high or doesn't drive it at all.

unasserted: For an active-low signal, synonymous with high, deasserted, false, inactive, and released.

word: As used in Part I of this book, a NuBus word is 32-bits long; a halfword, 16-bits. As used in Part II of this book, word refers to an SE-Bus or MC68000 word and is 16-bits long; a halfword is 8-bits.

Index